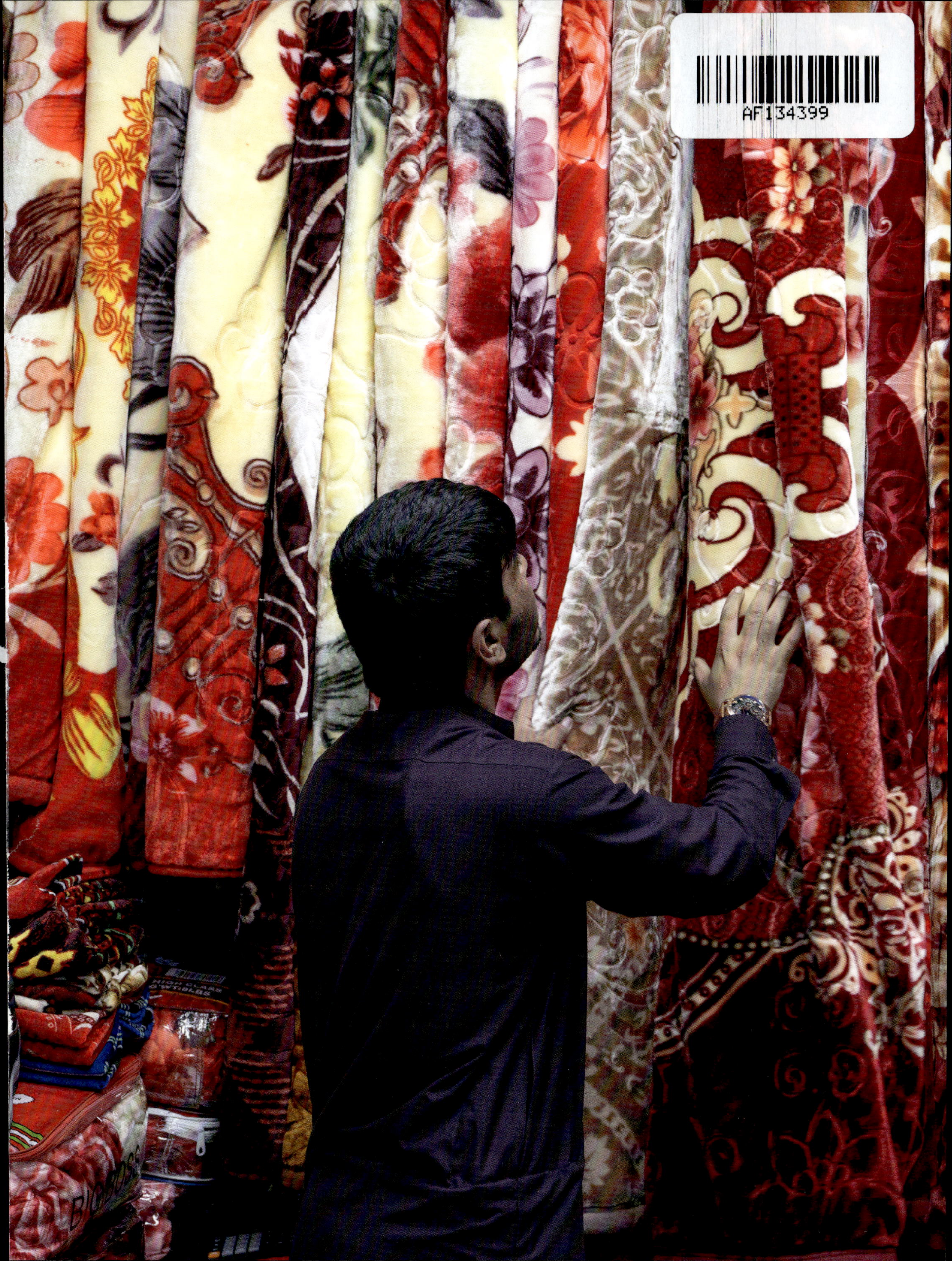

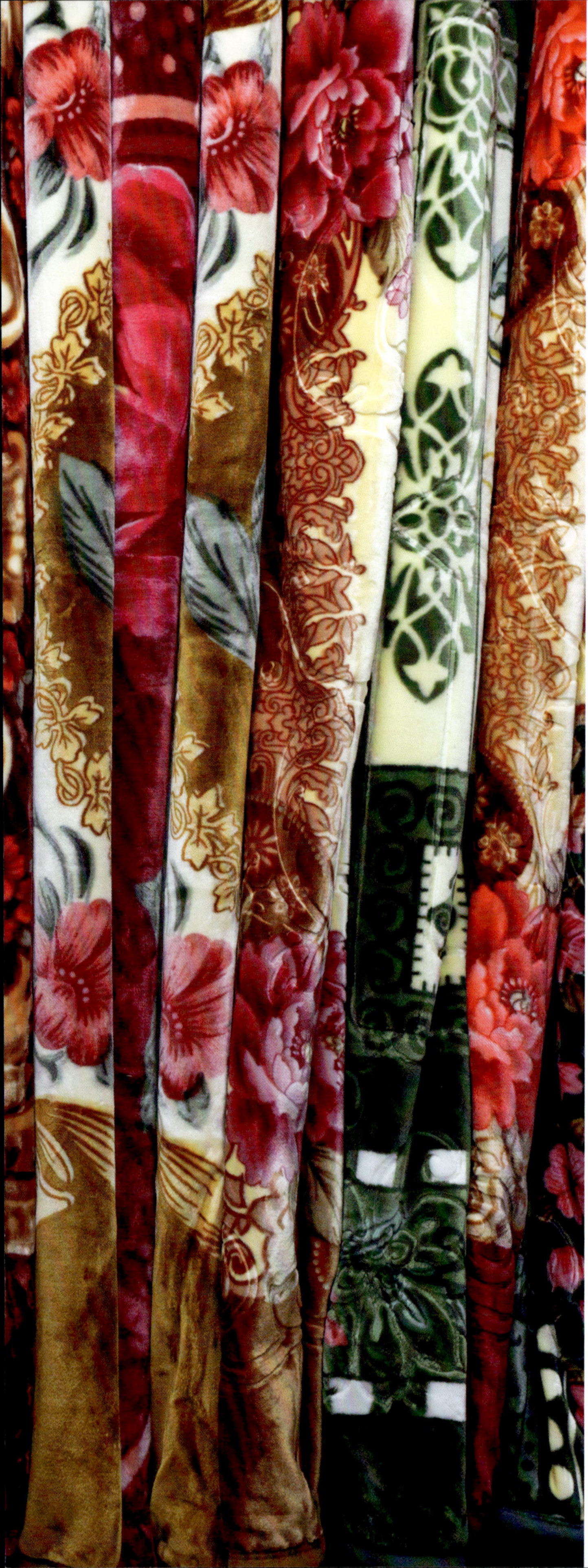

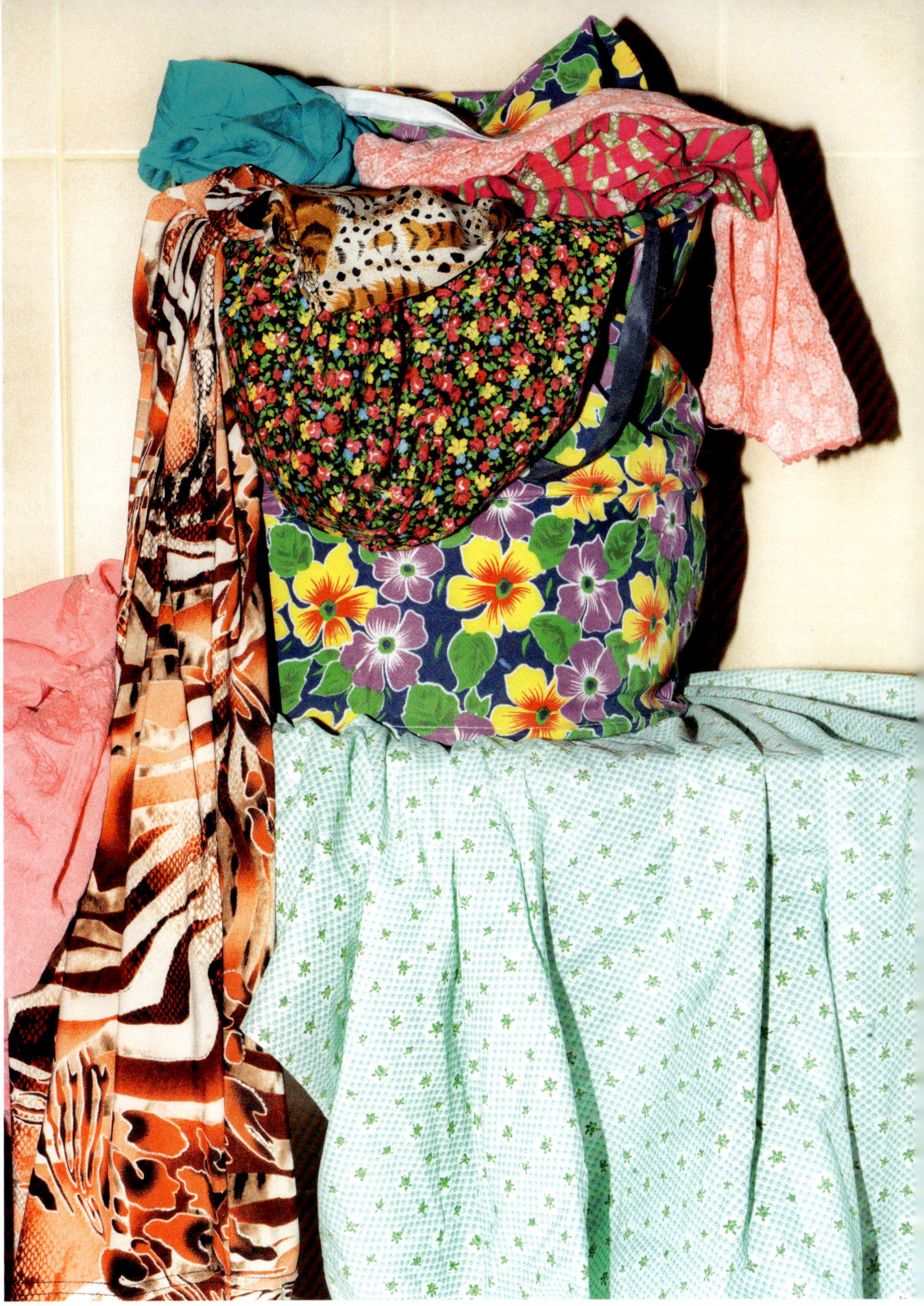

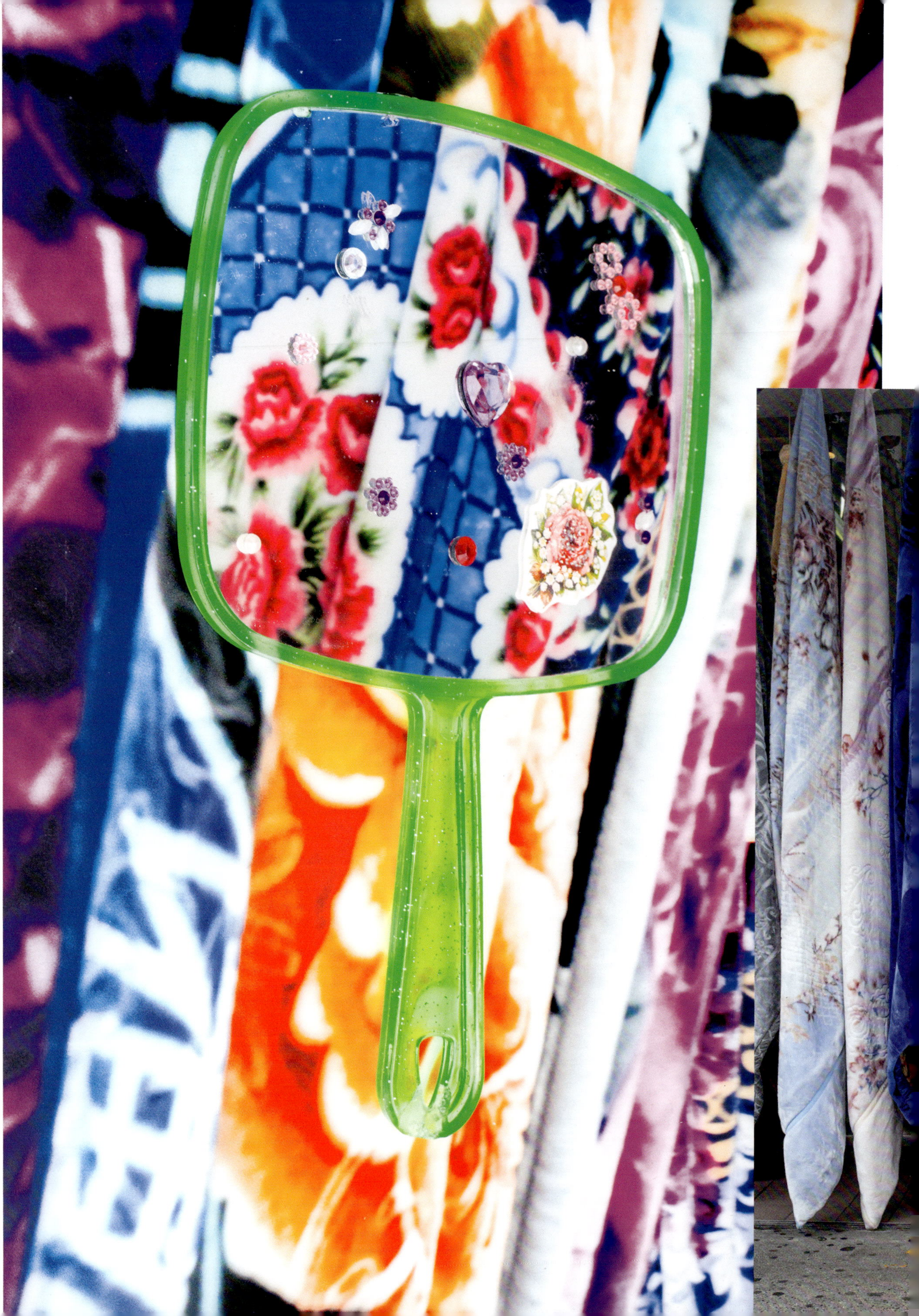

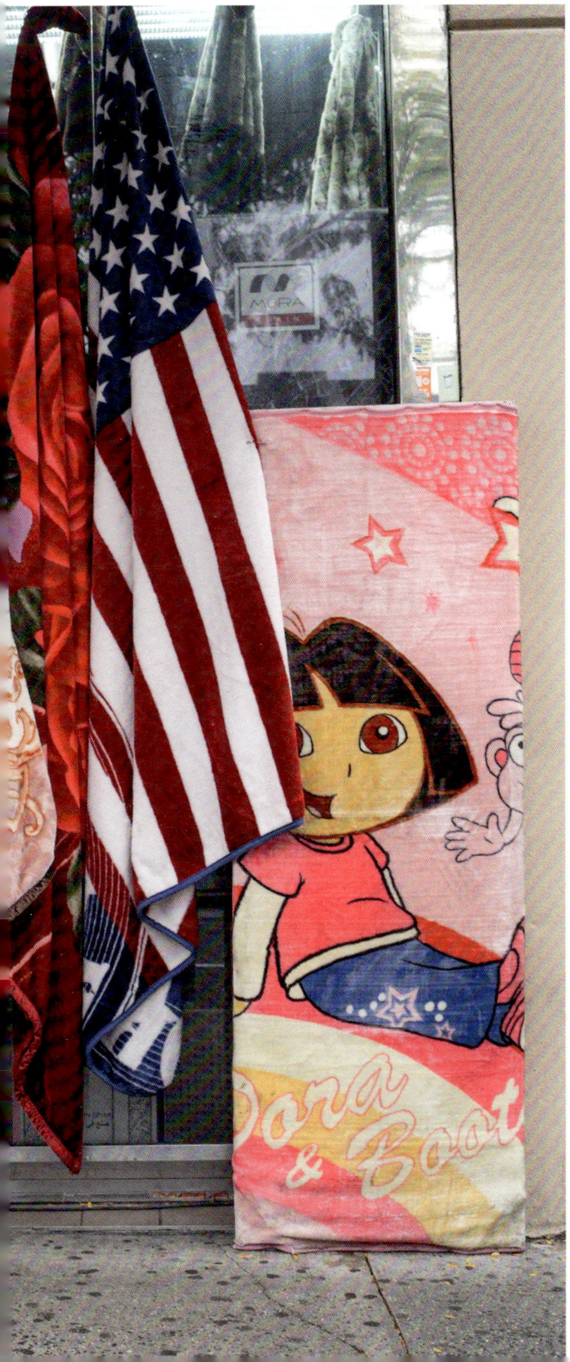
MORA
Dora
& Boot

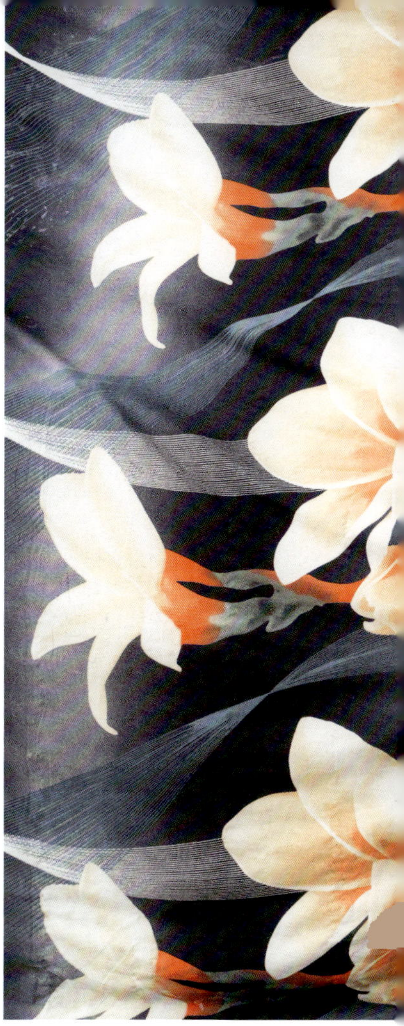

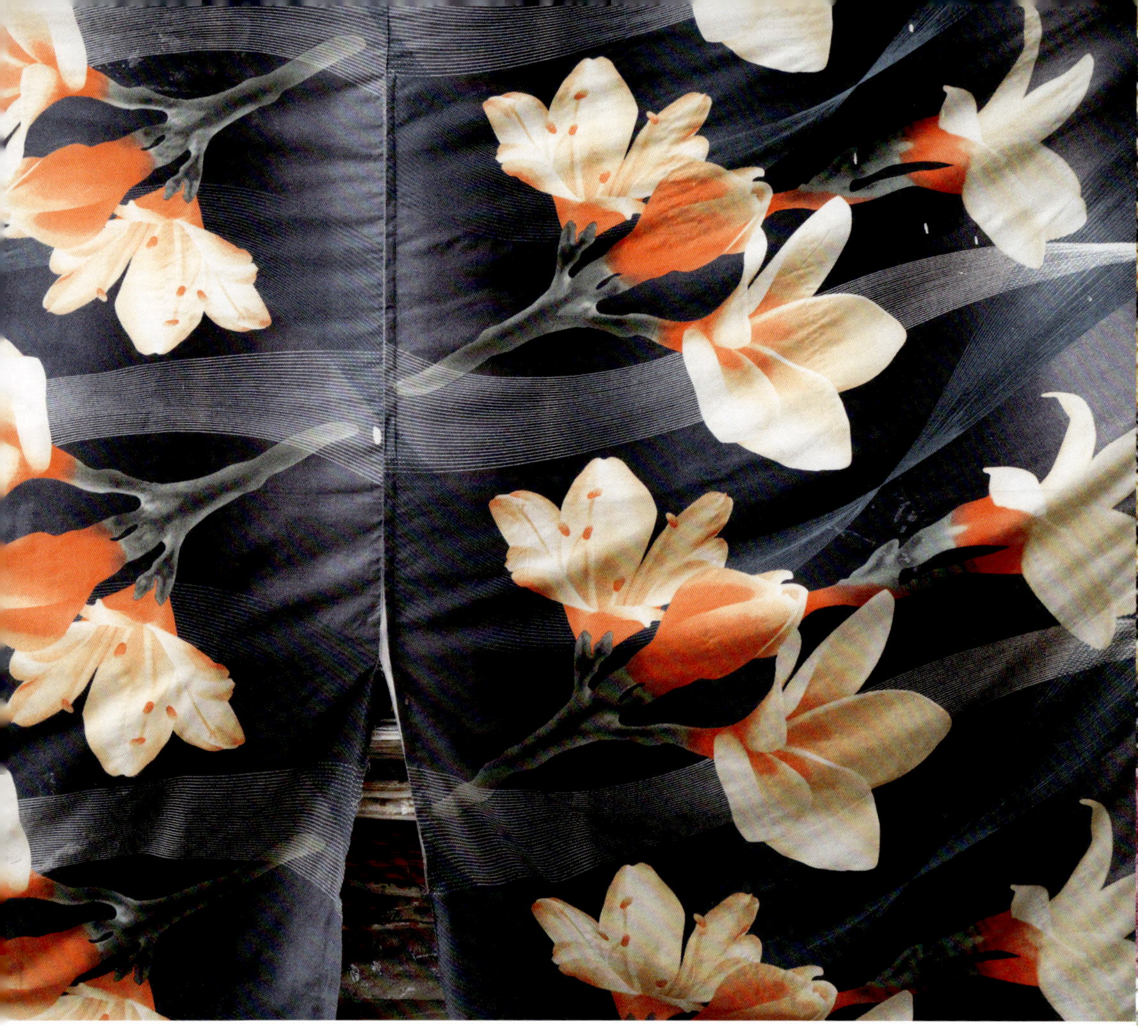

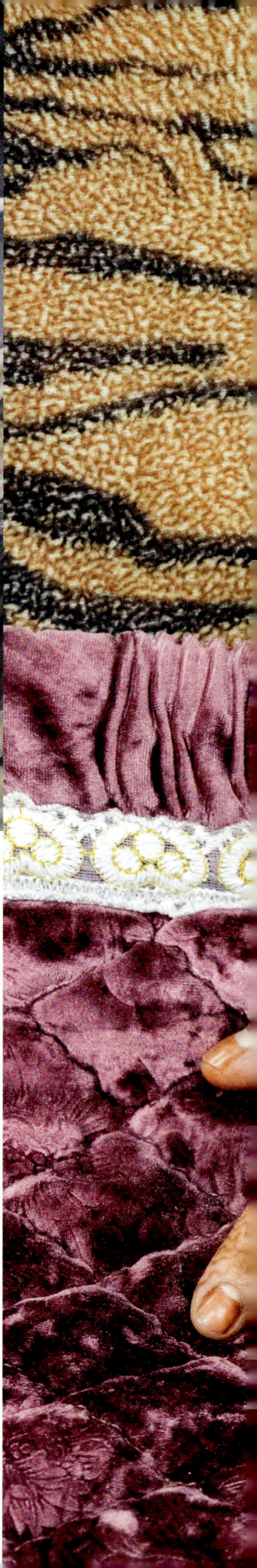

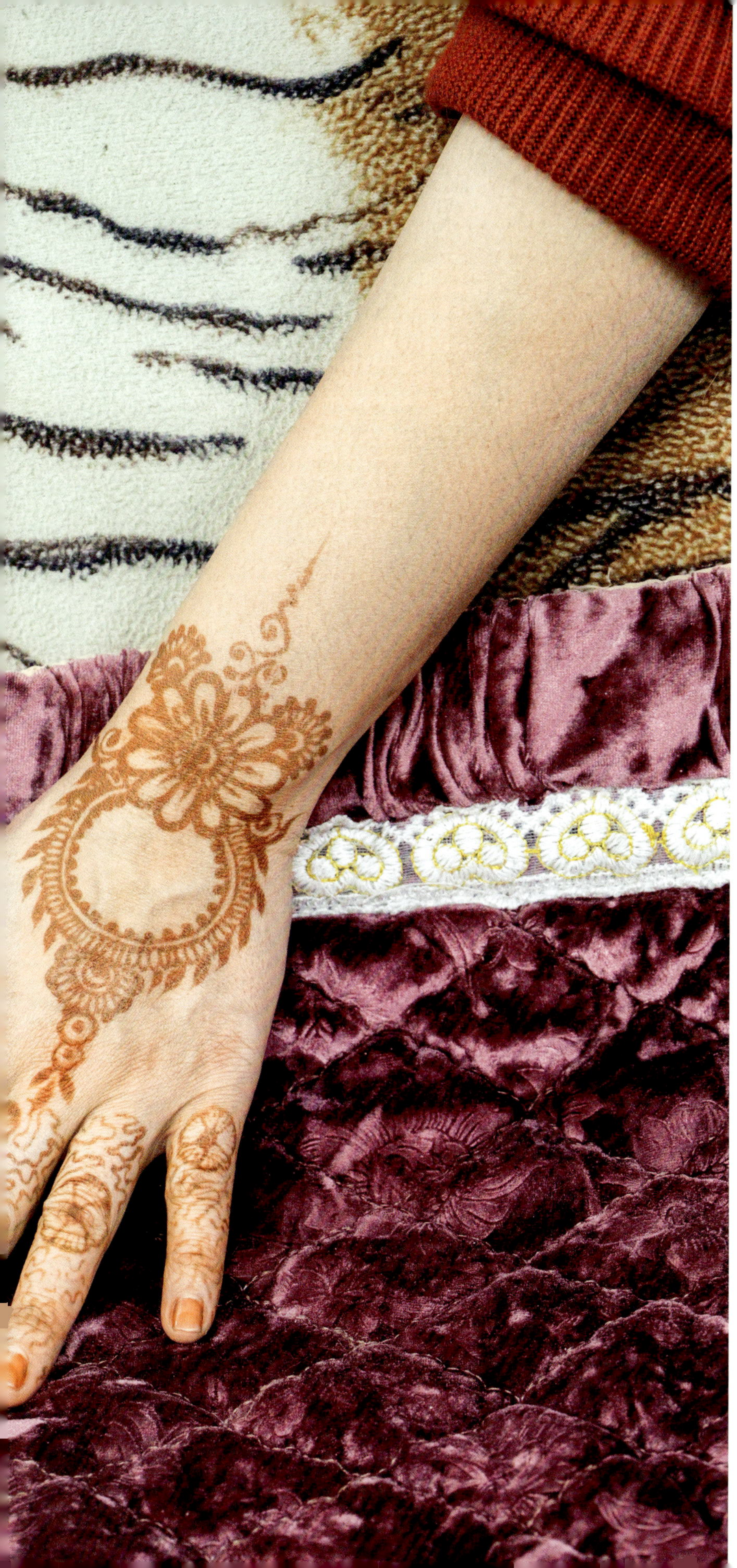

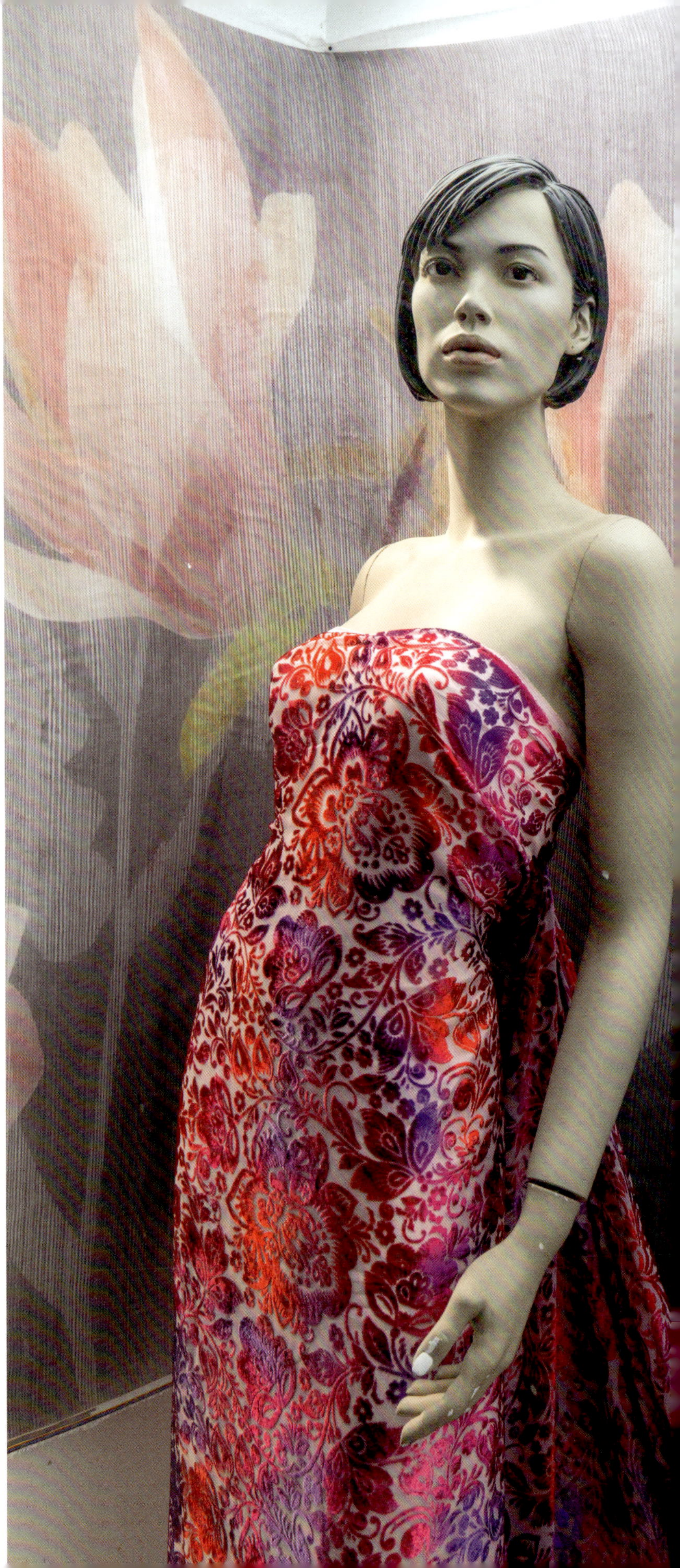

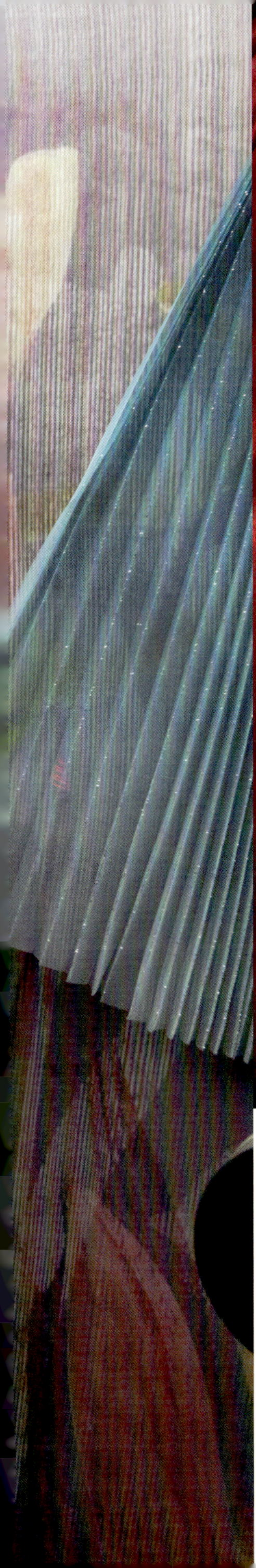

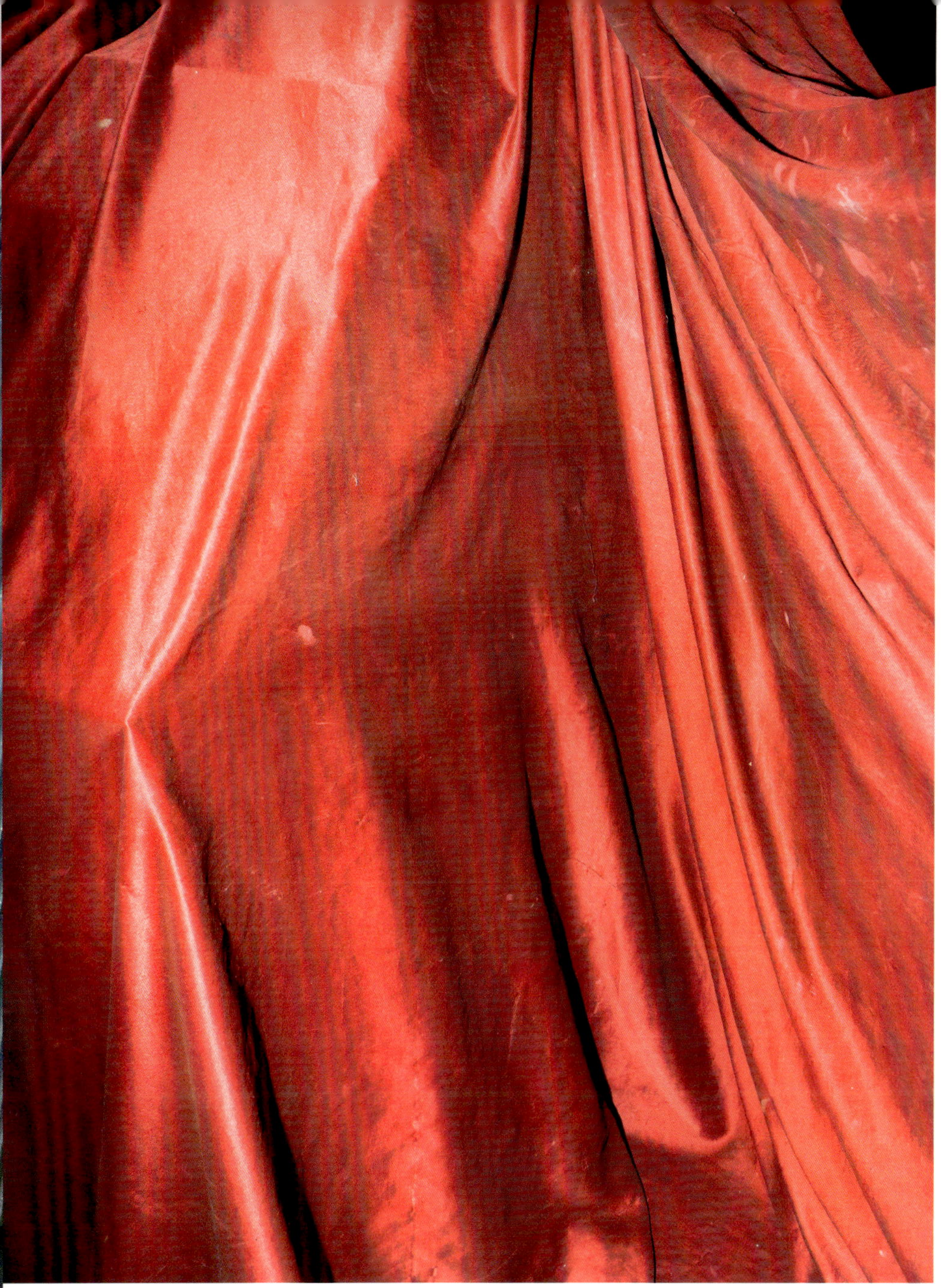

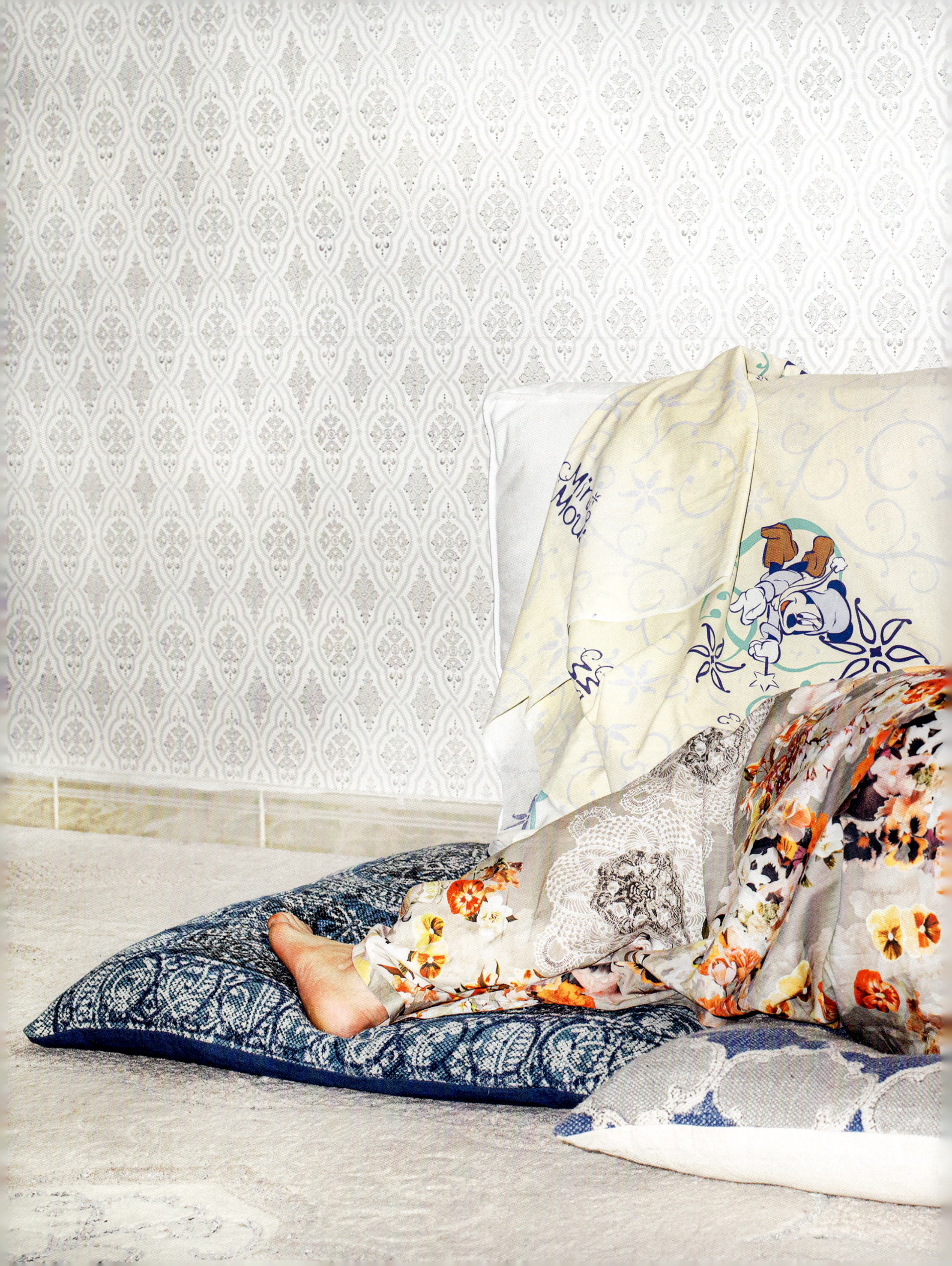

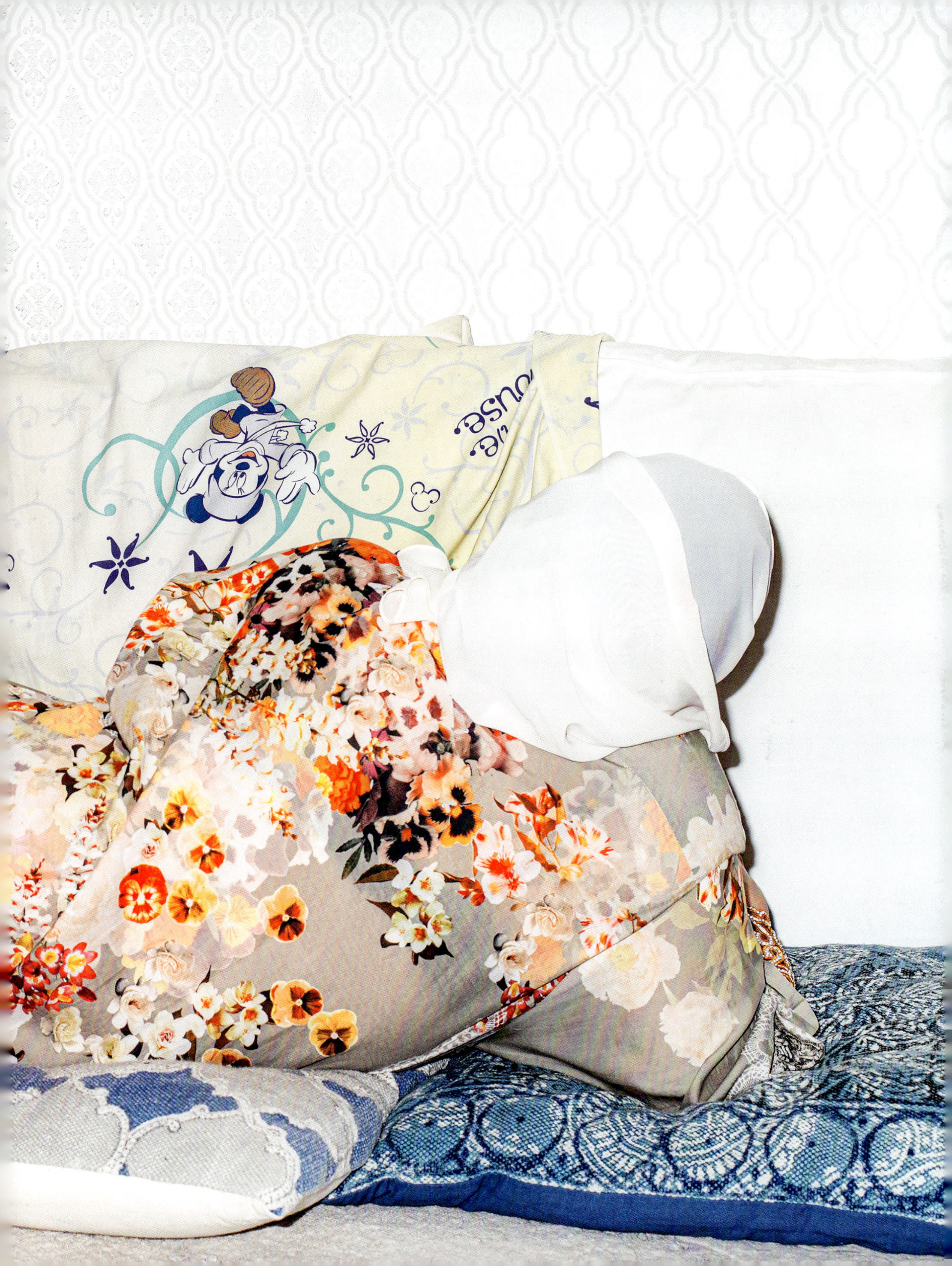

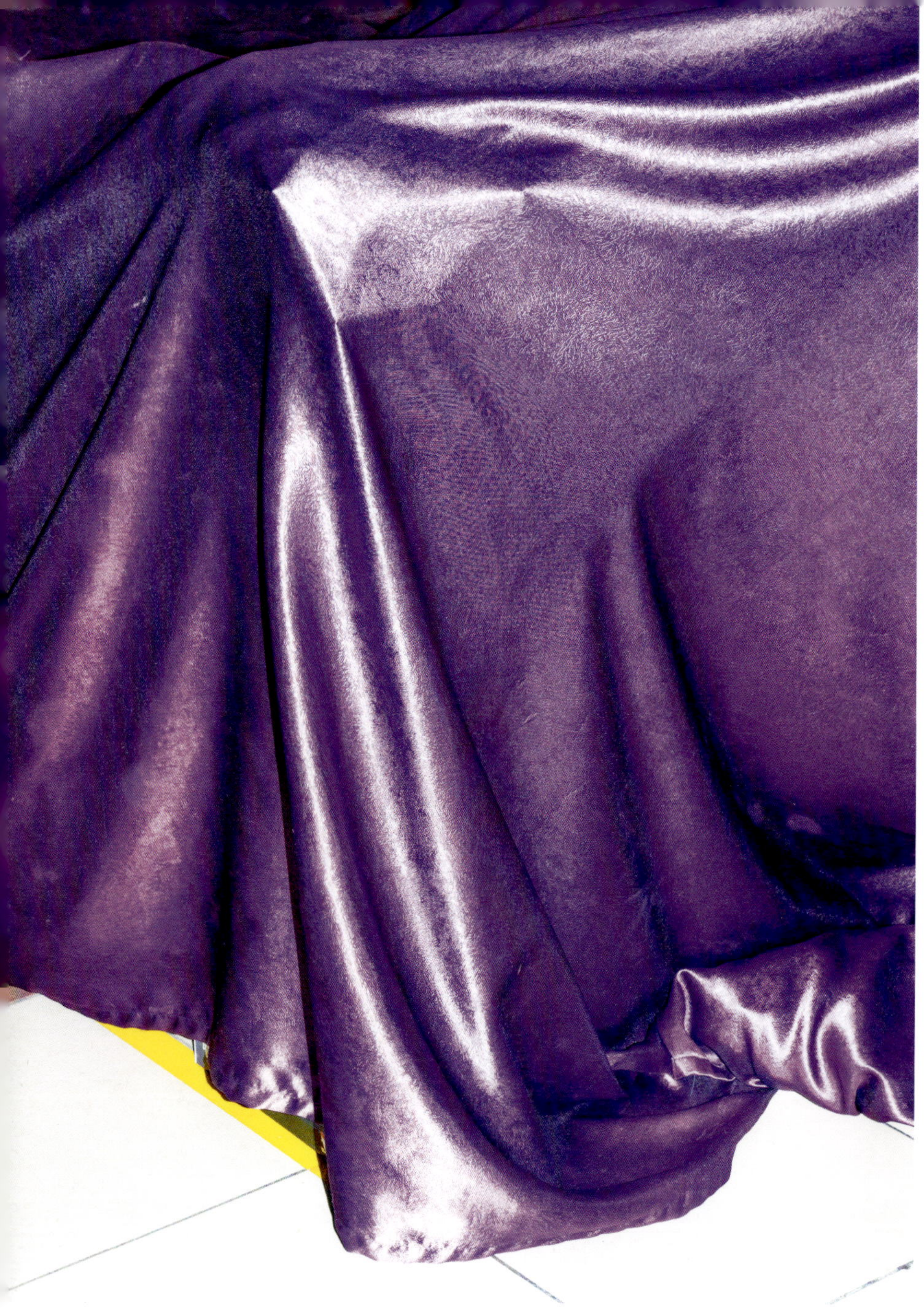

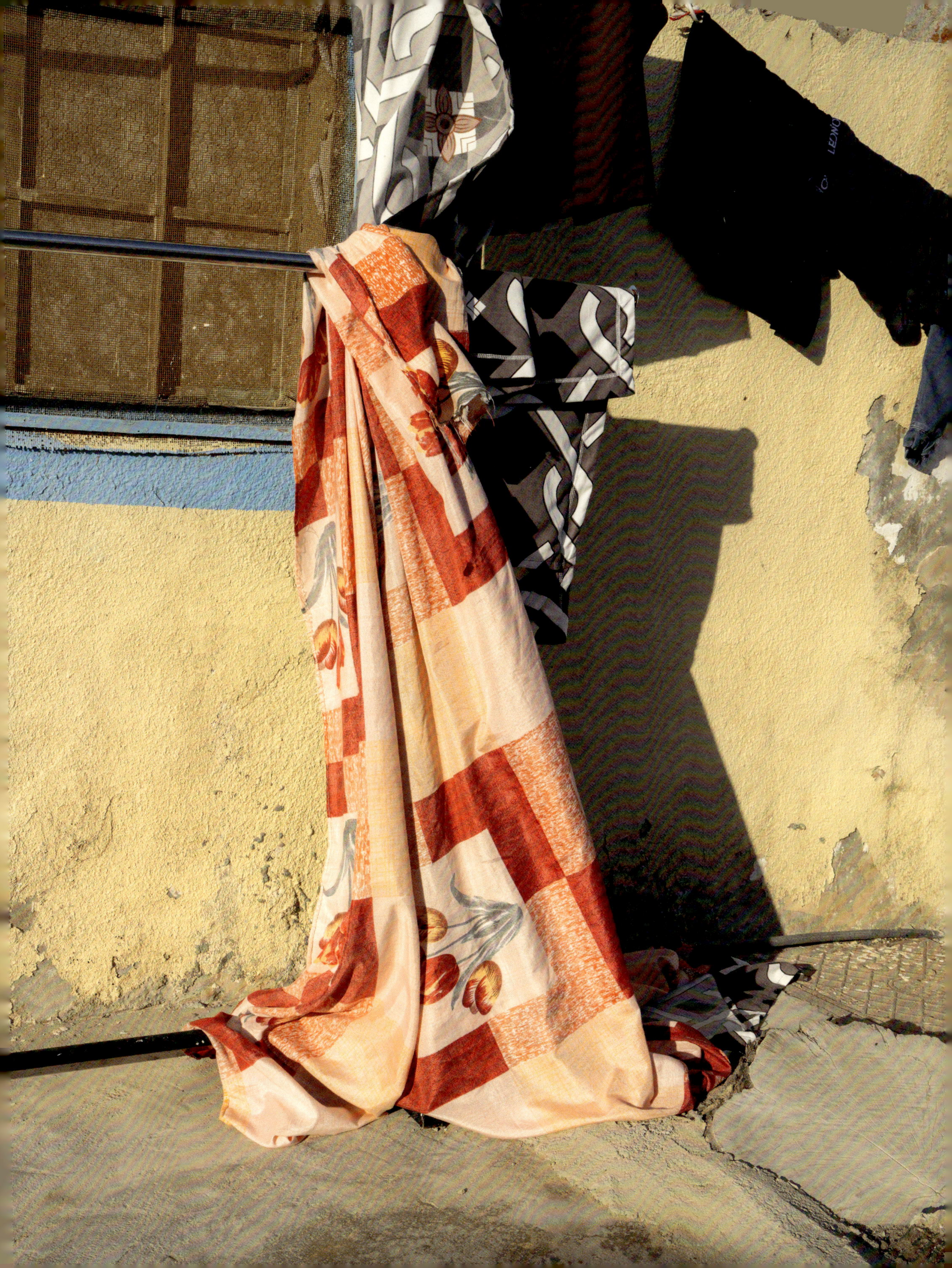

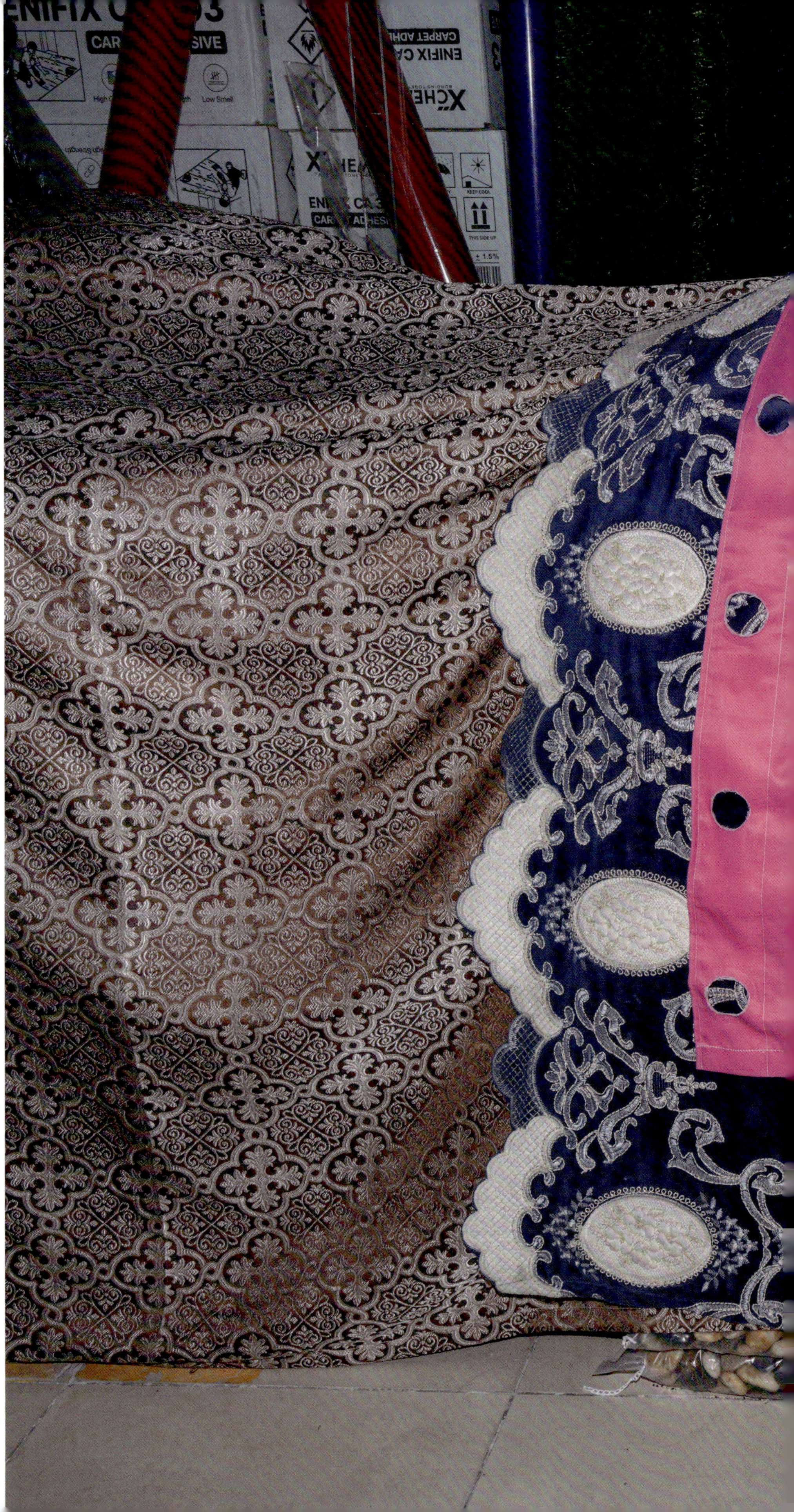
Low Smell

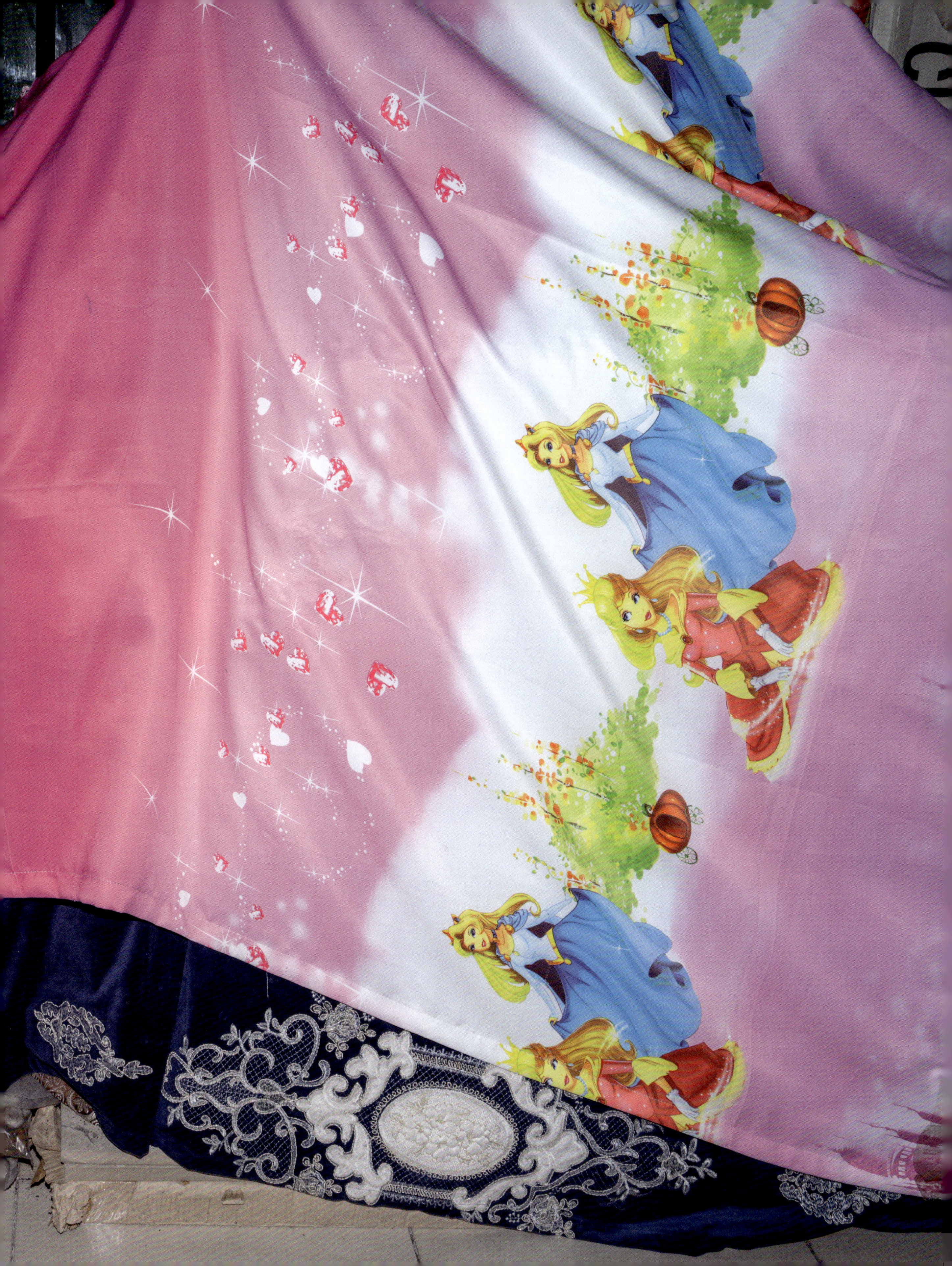

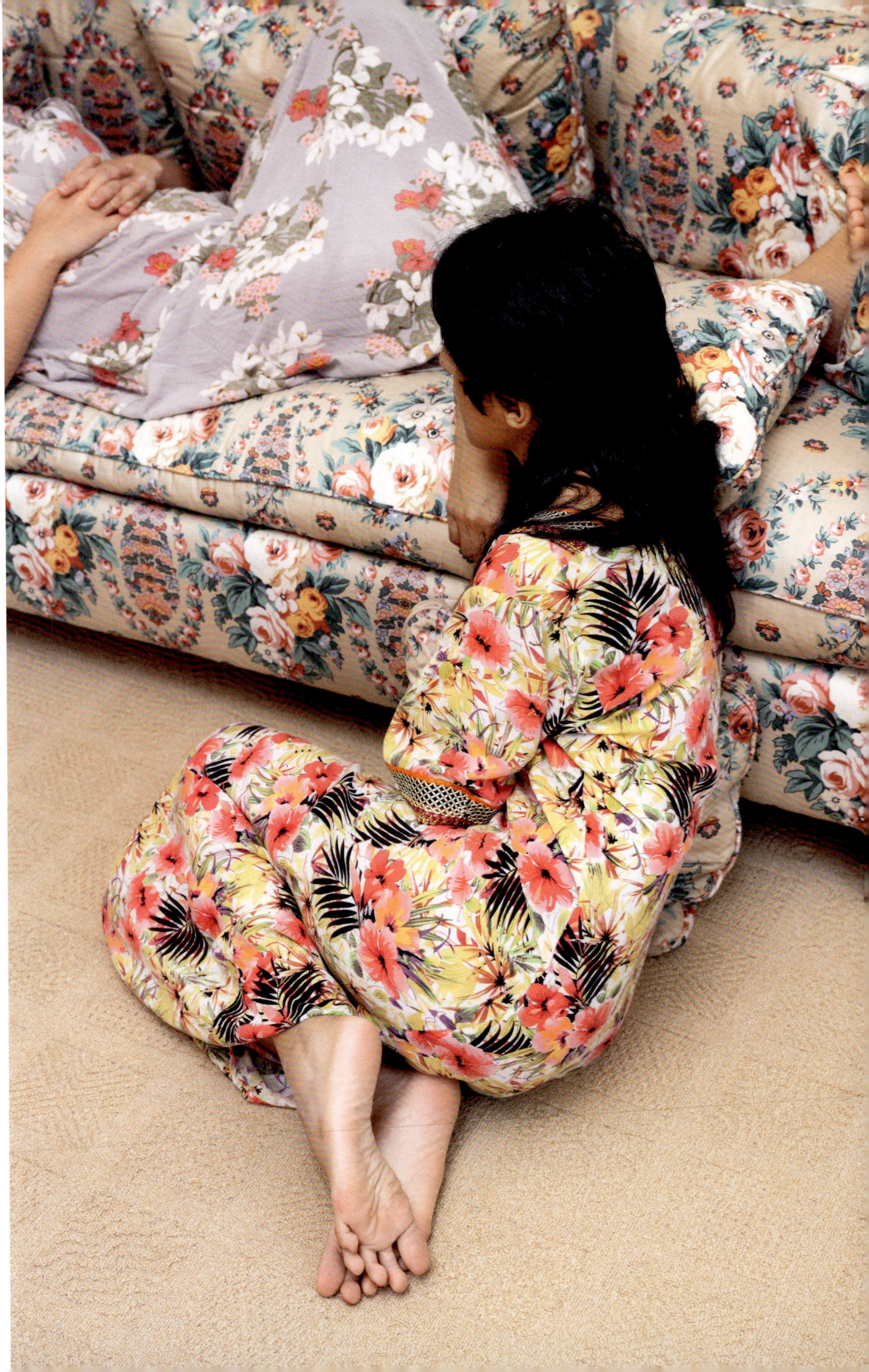

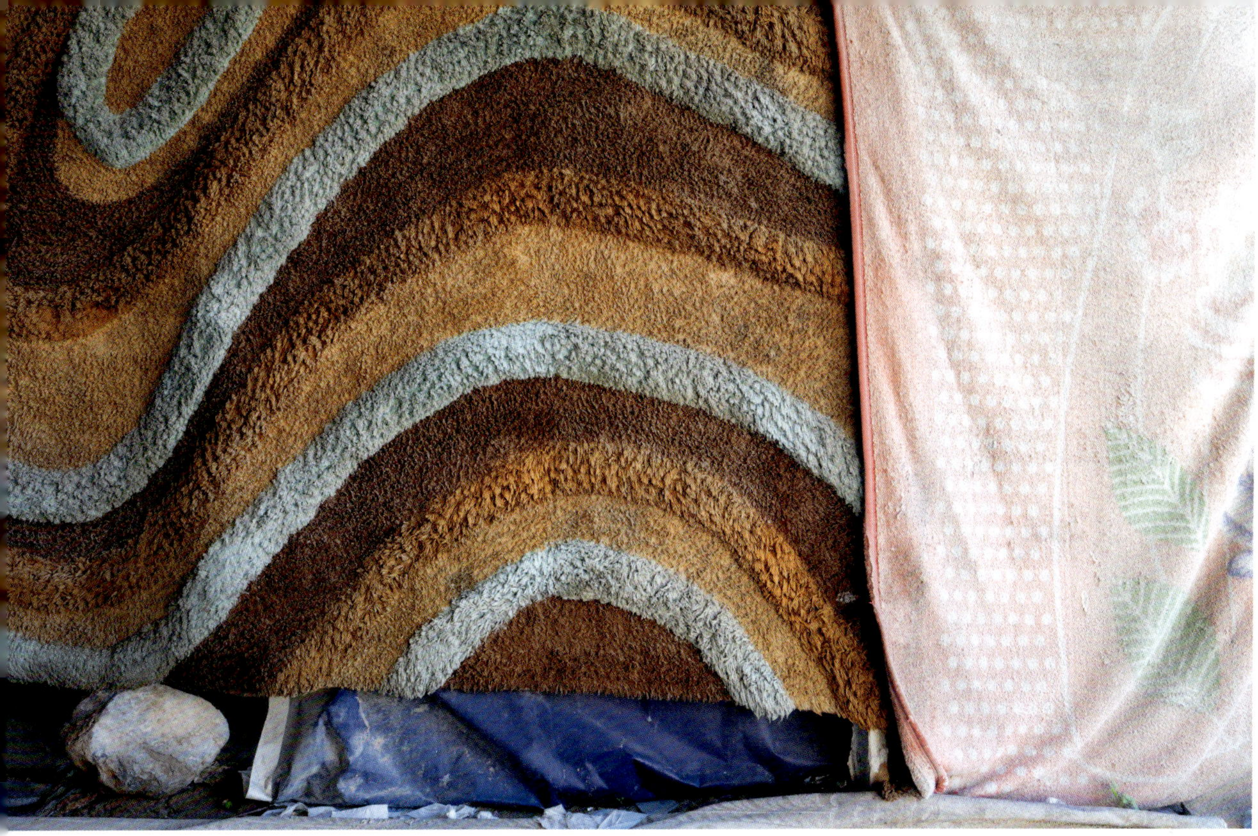

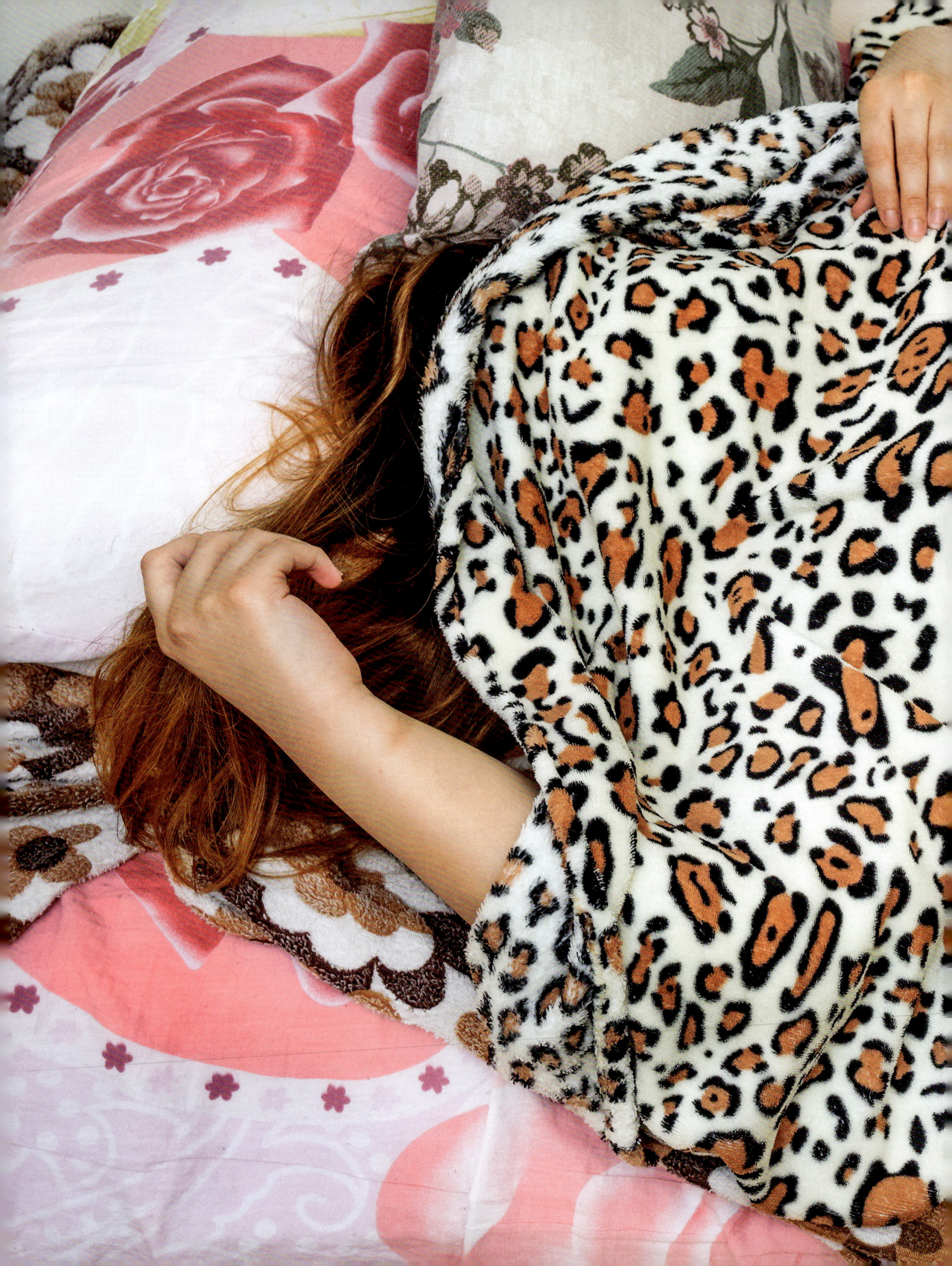

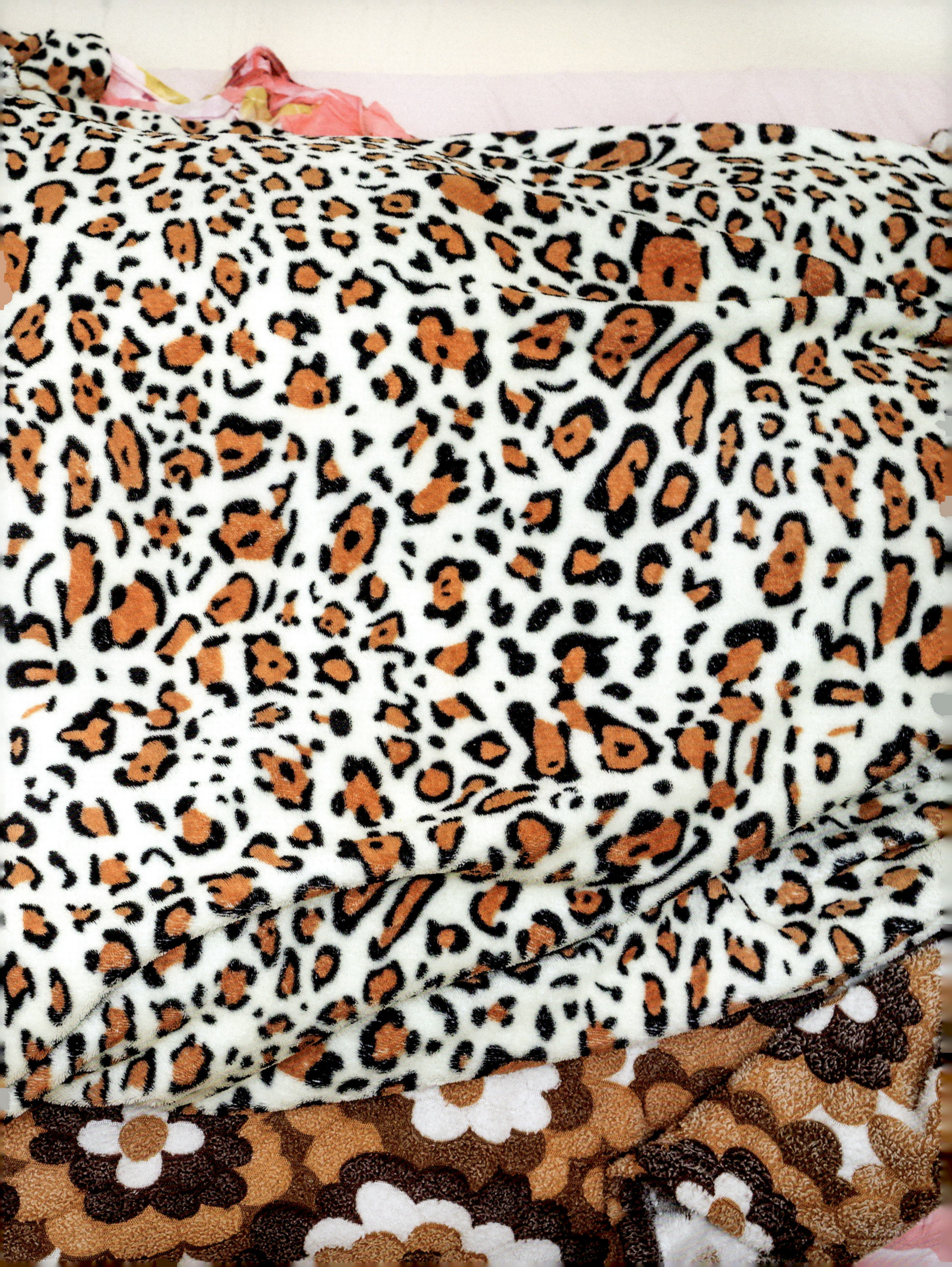

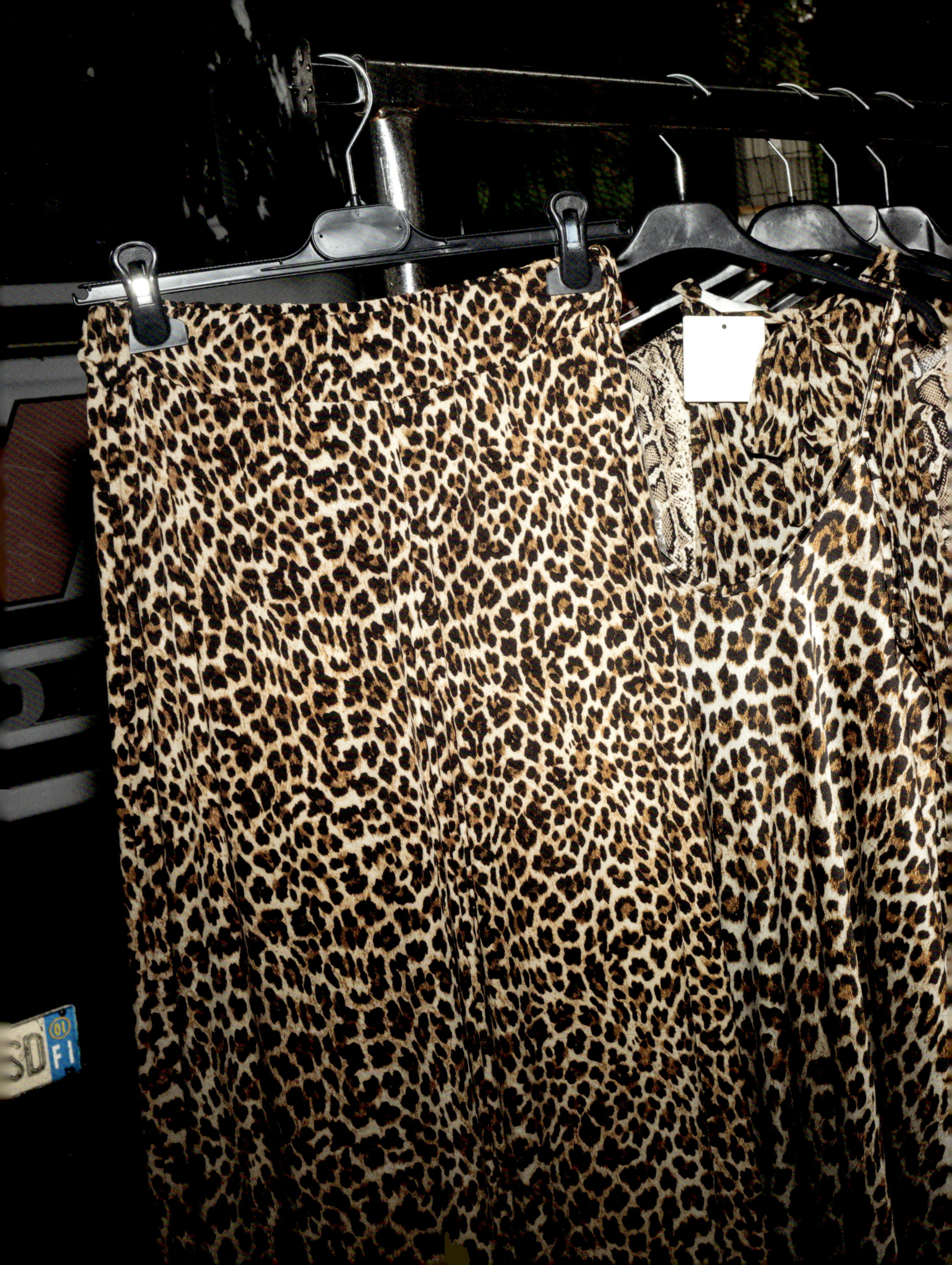

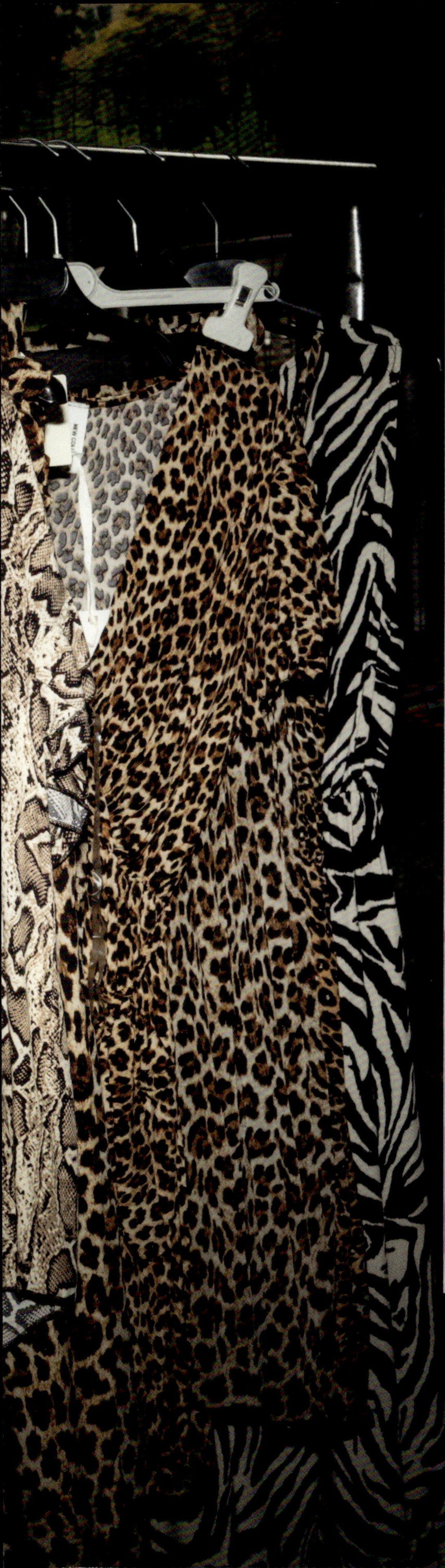
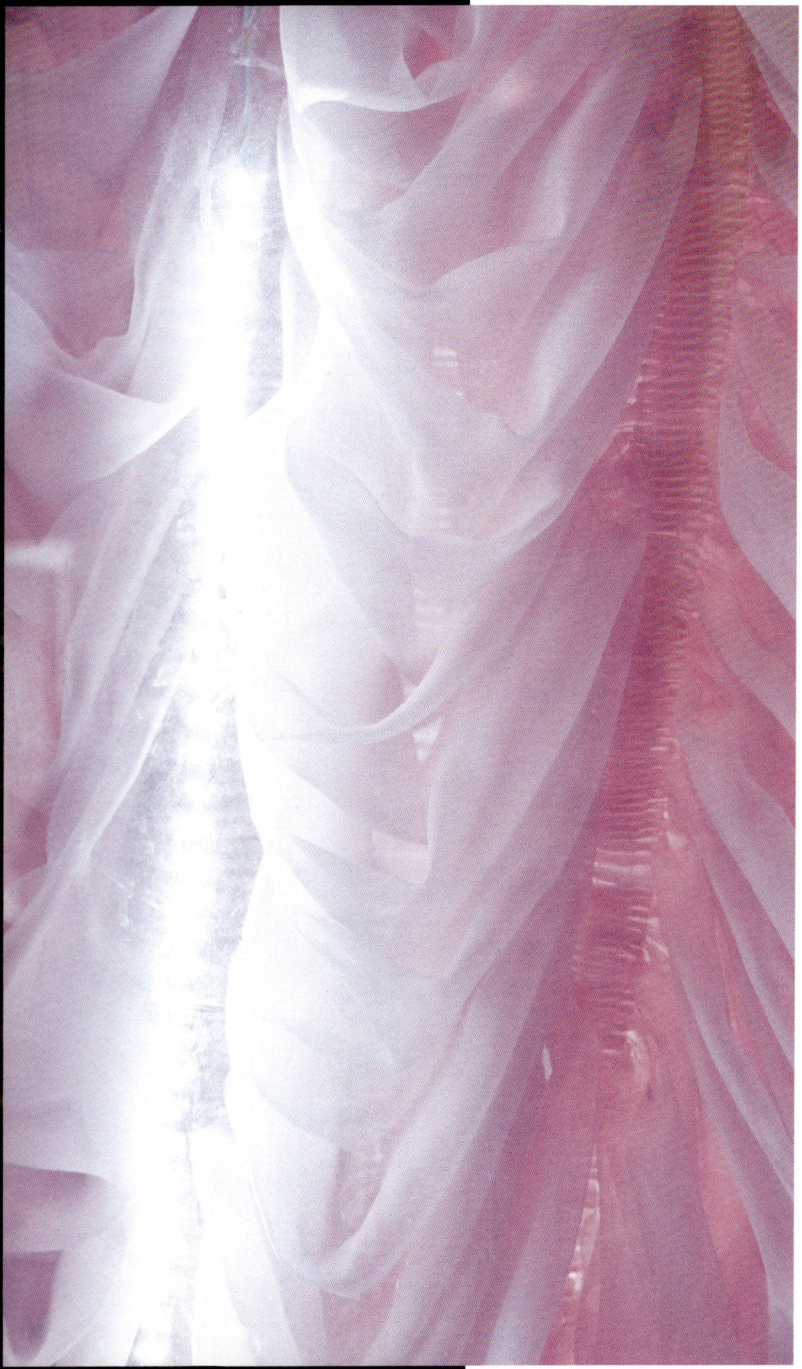

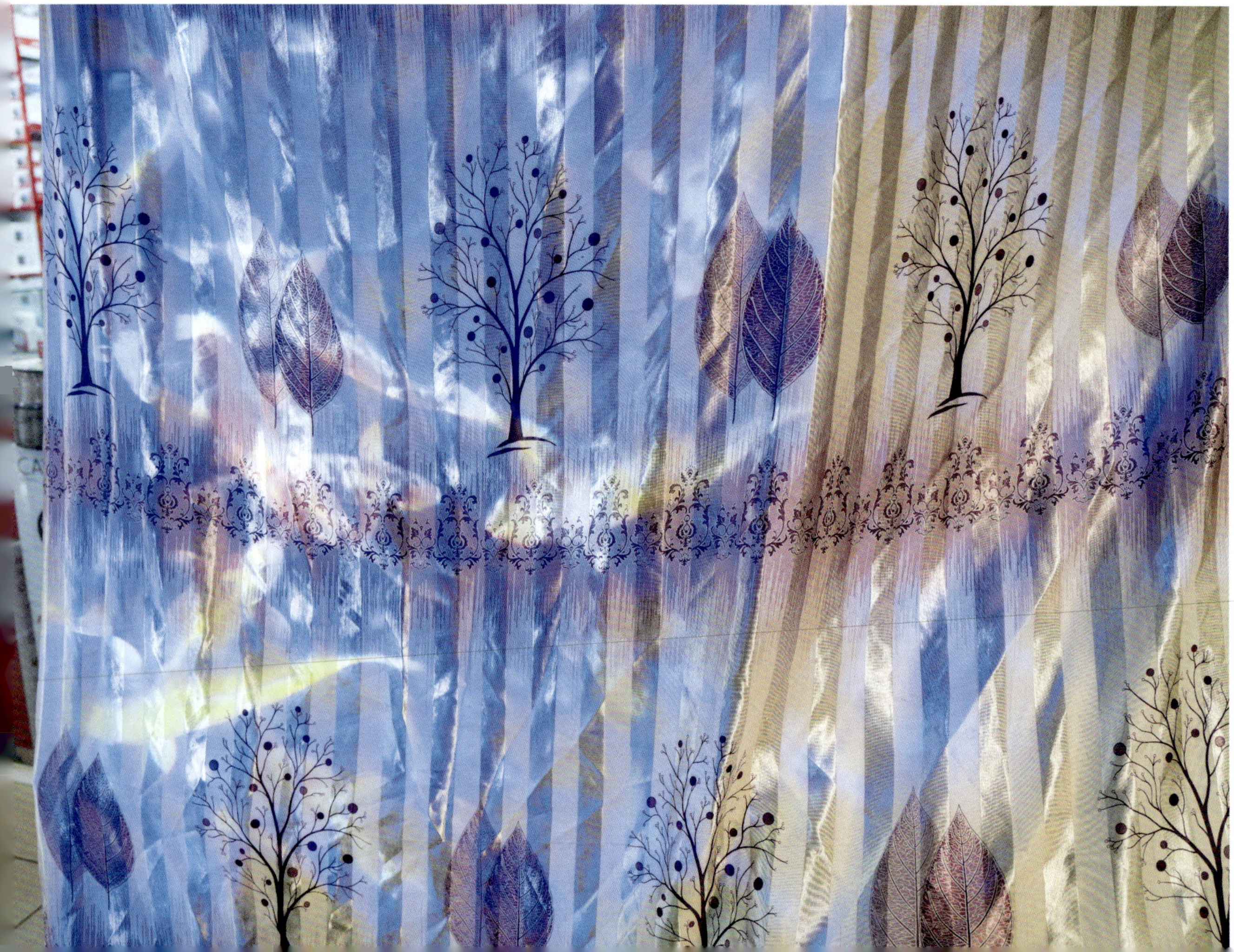

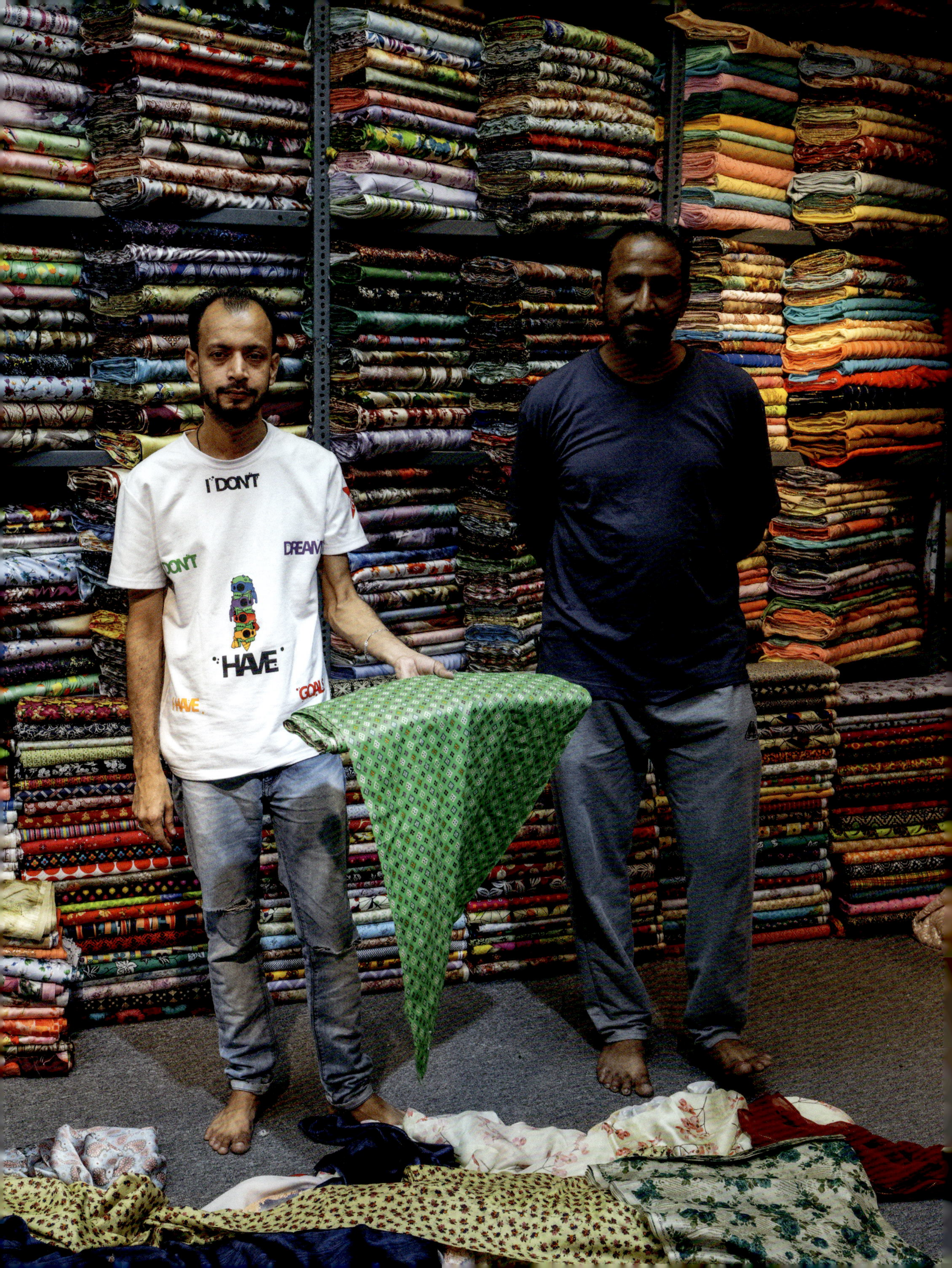
I DON'T
DON'T
HAVE

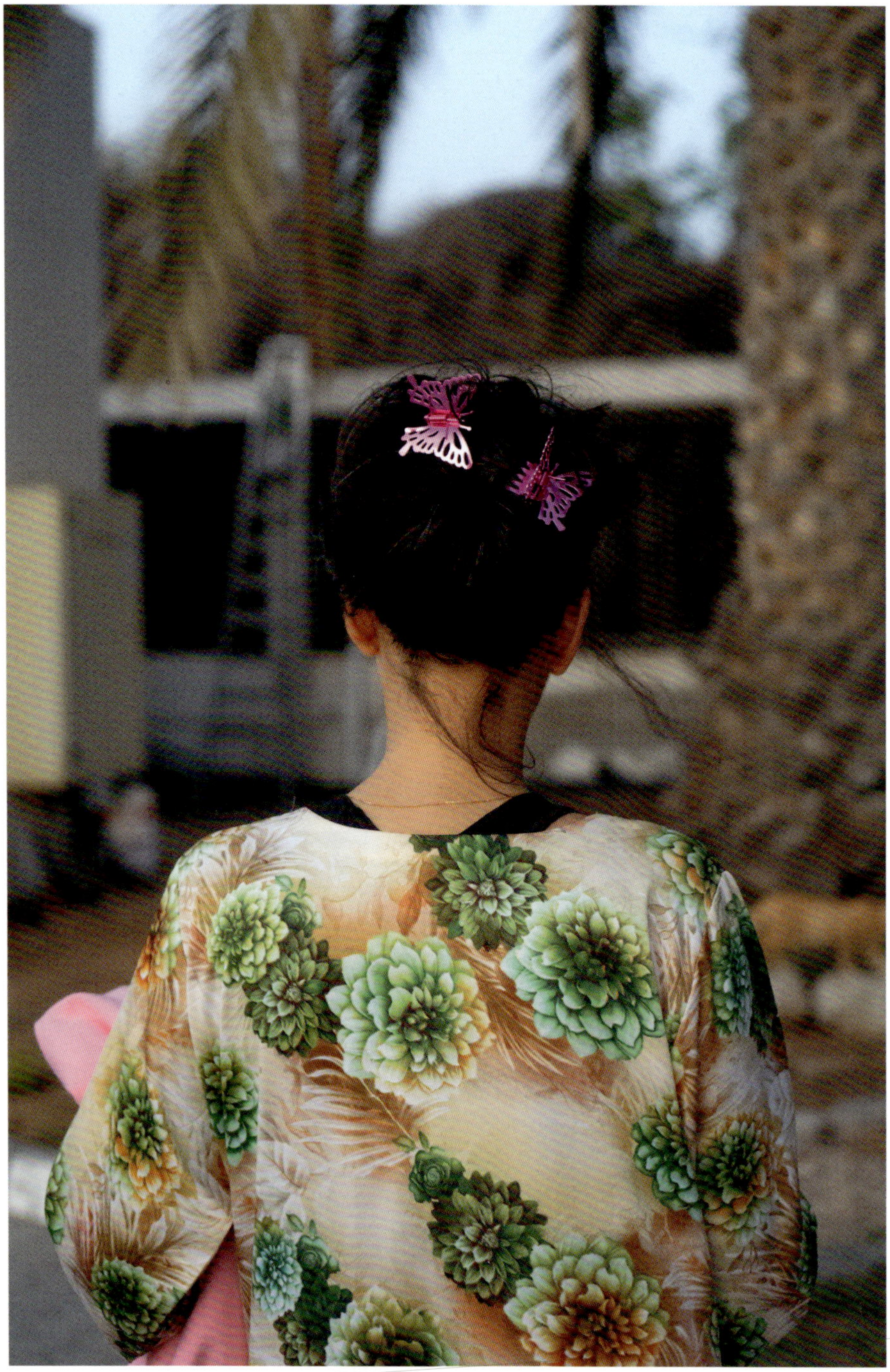

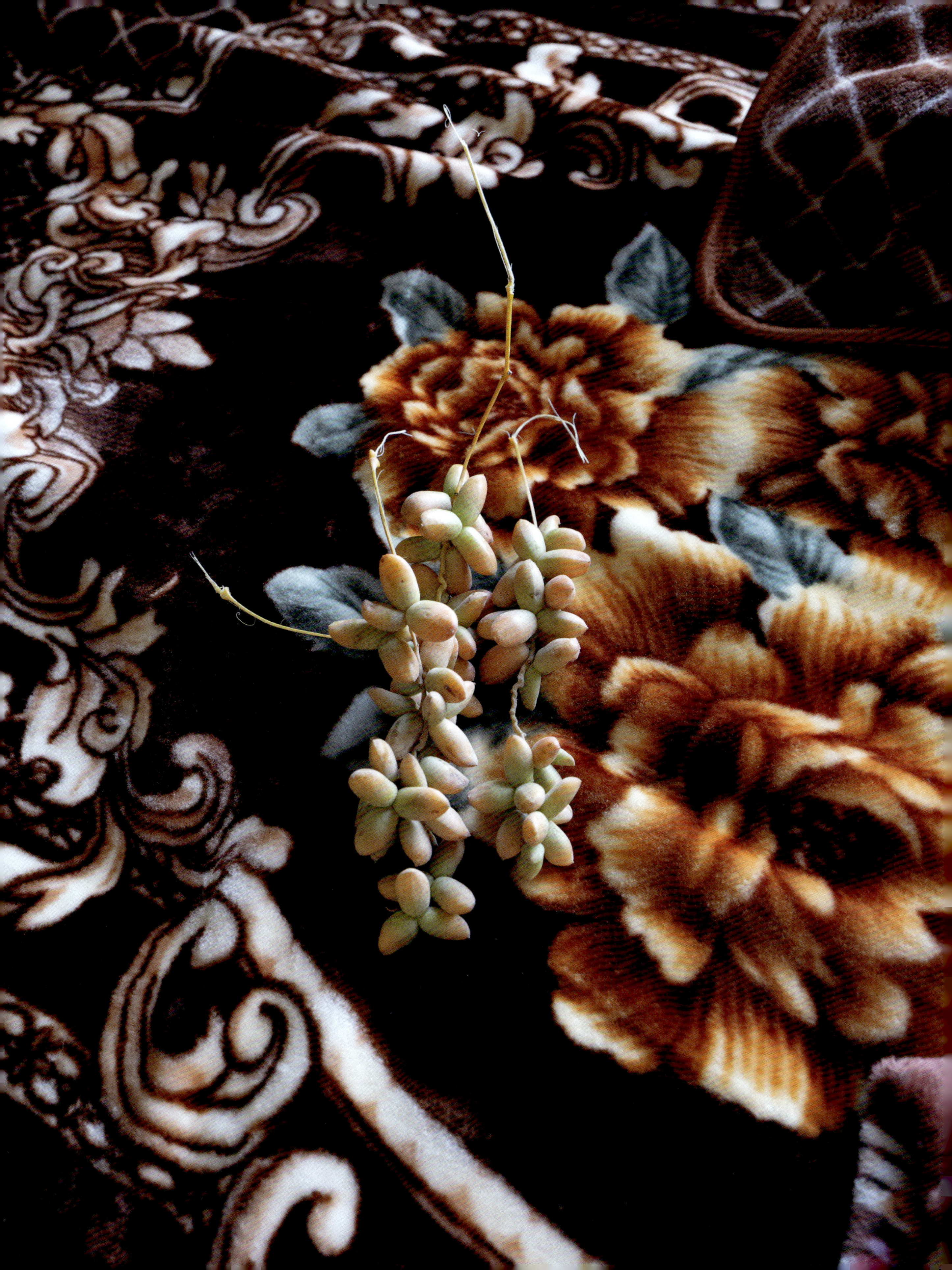

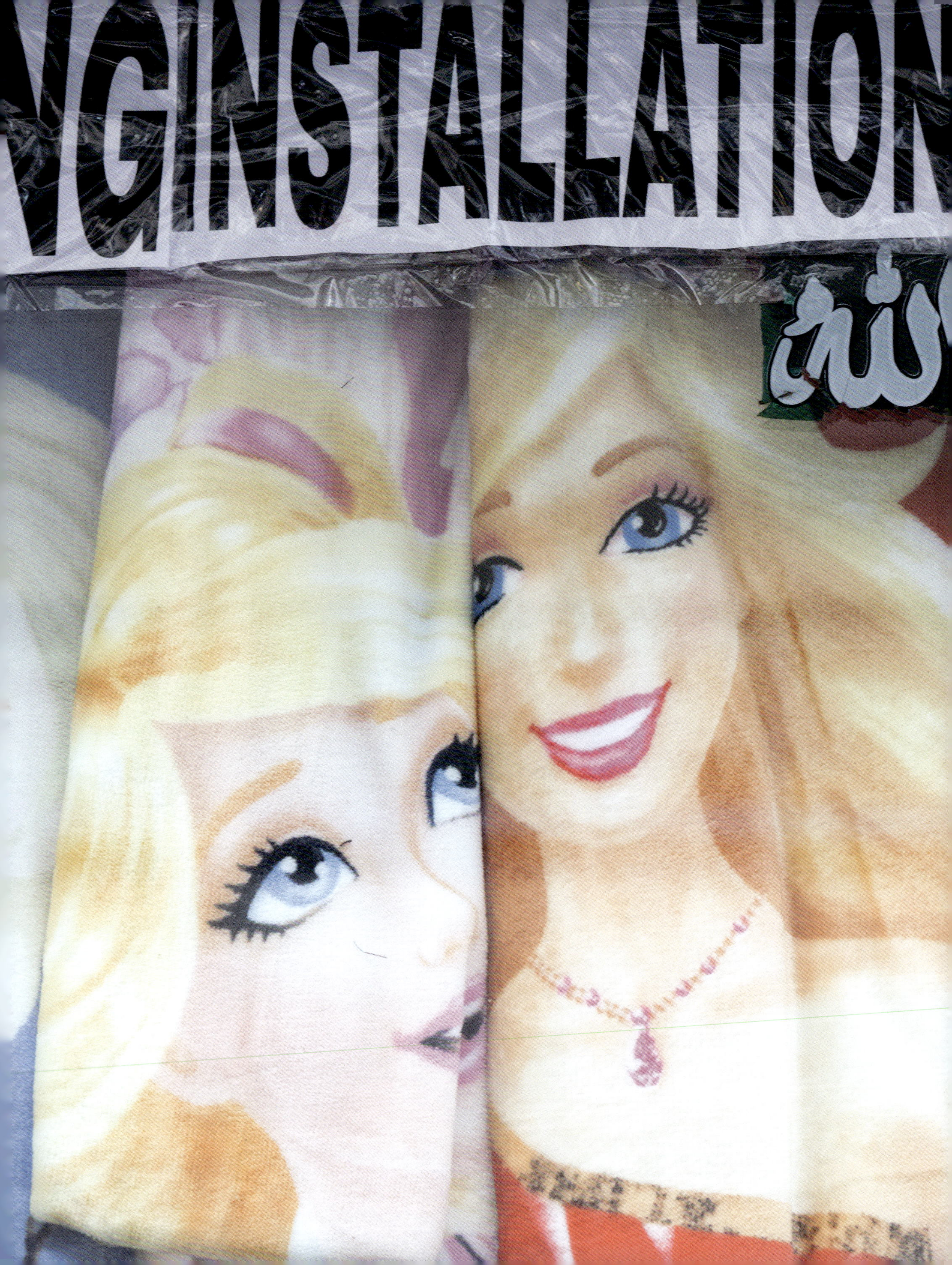
INSTALLATION
الله

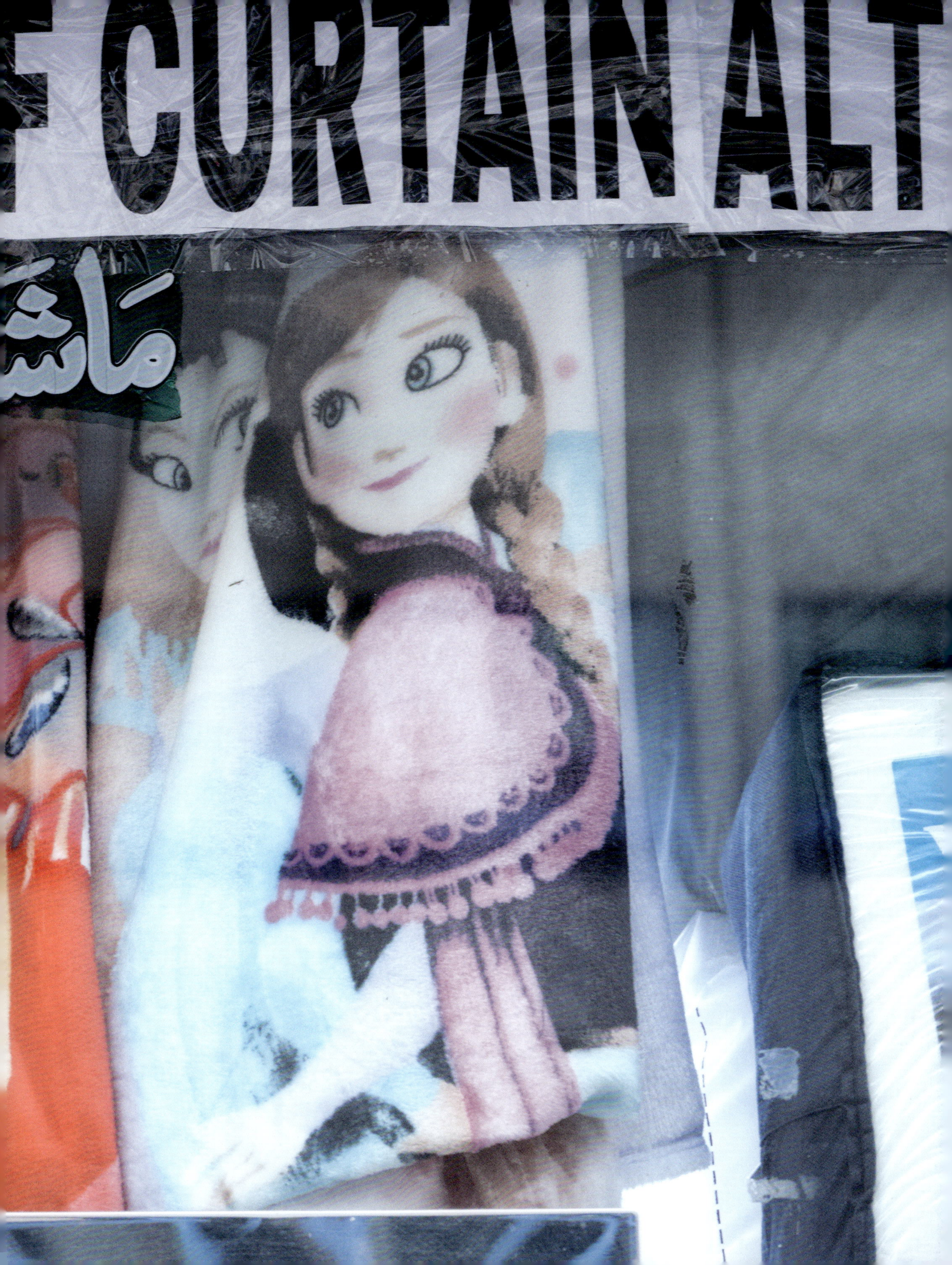
F CURTAIN ALT

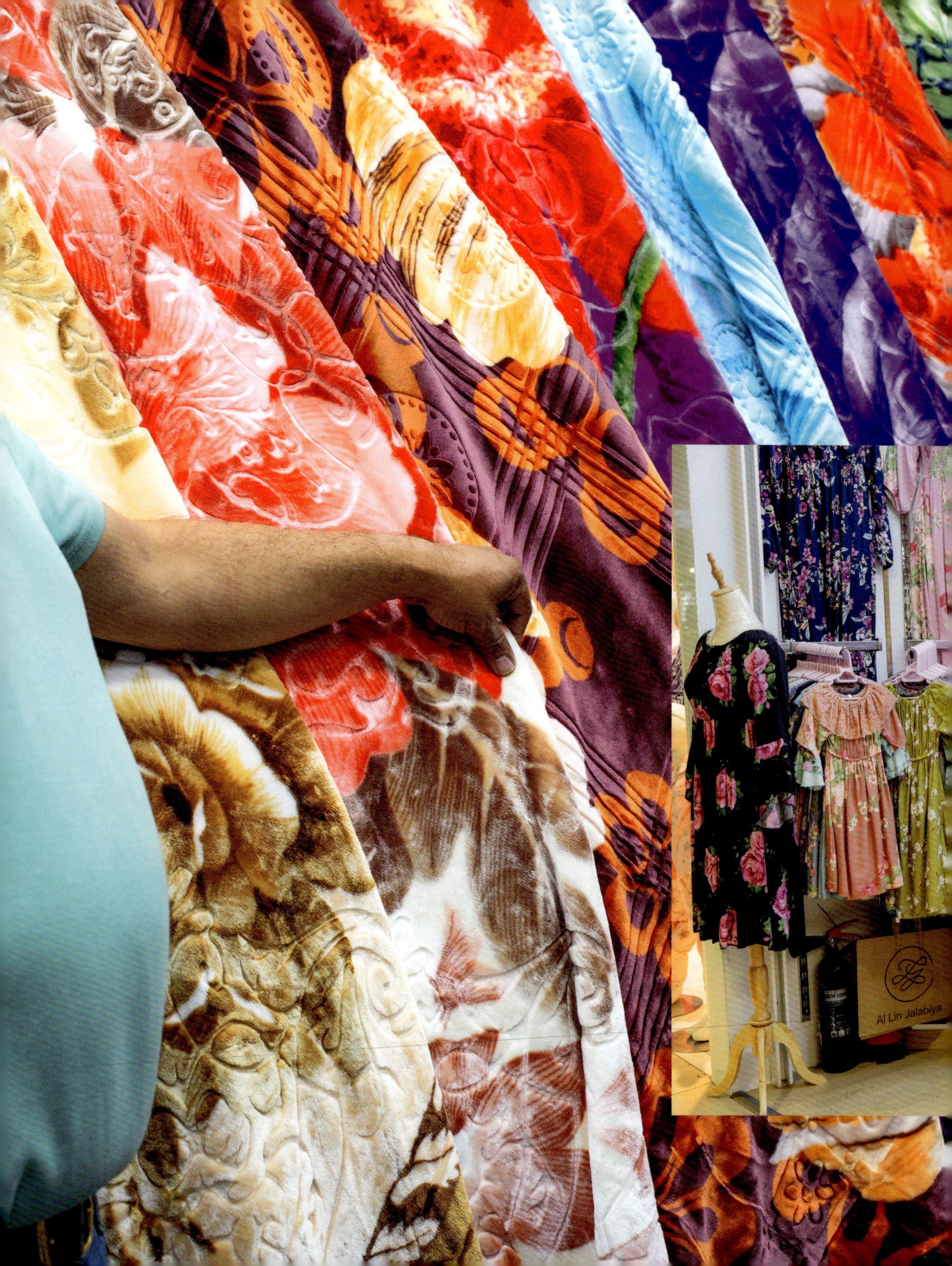
Al Lin Jalabiya

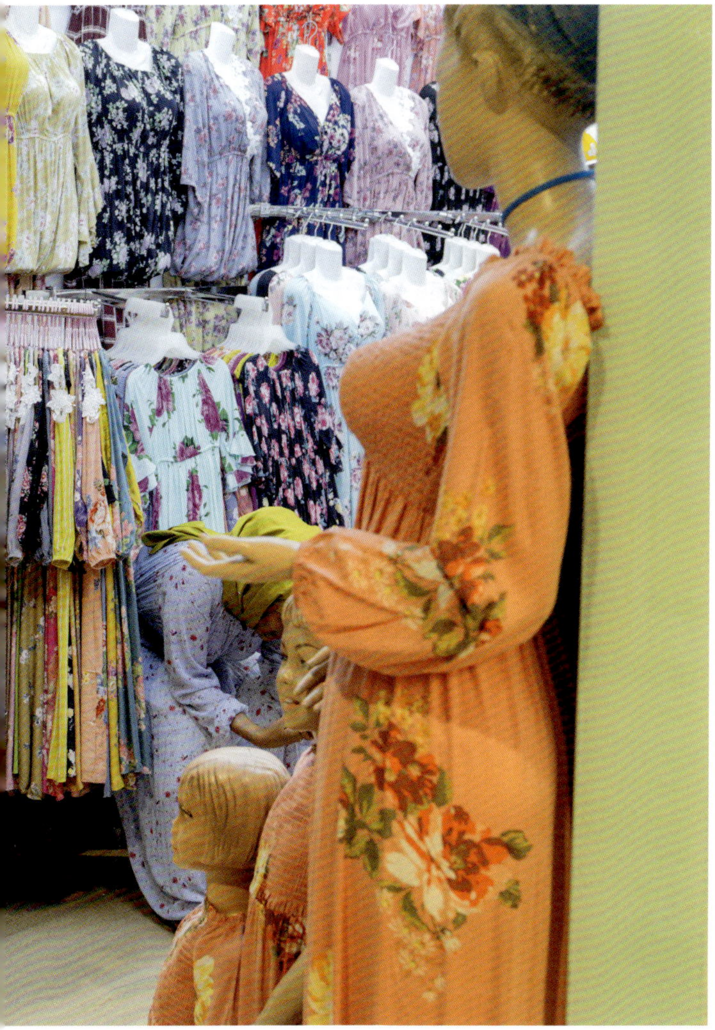

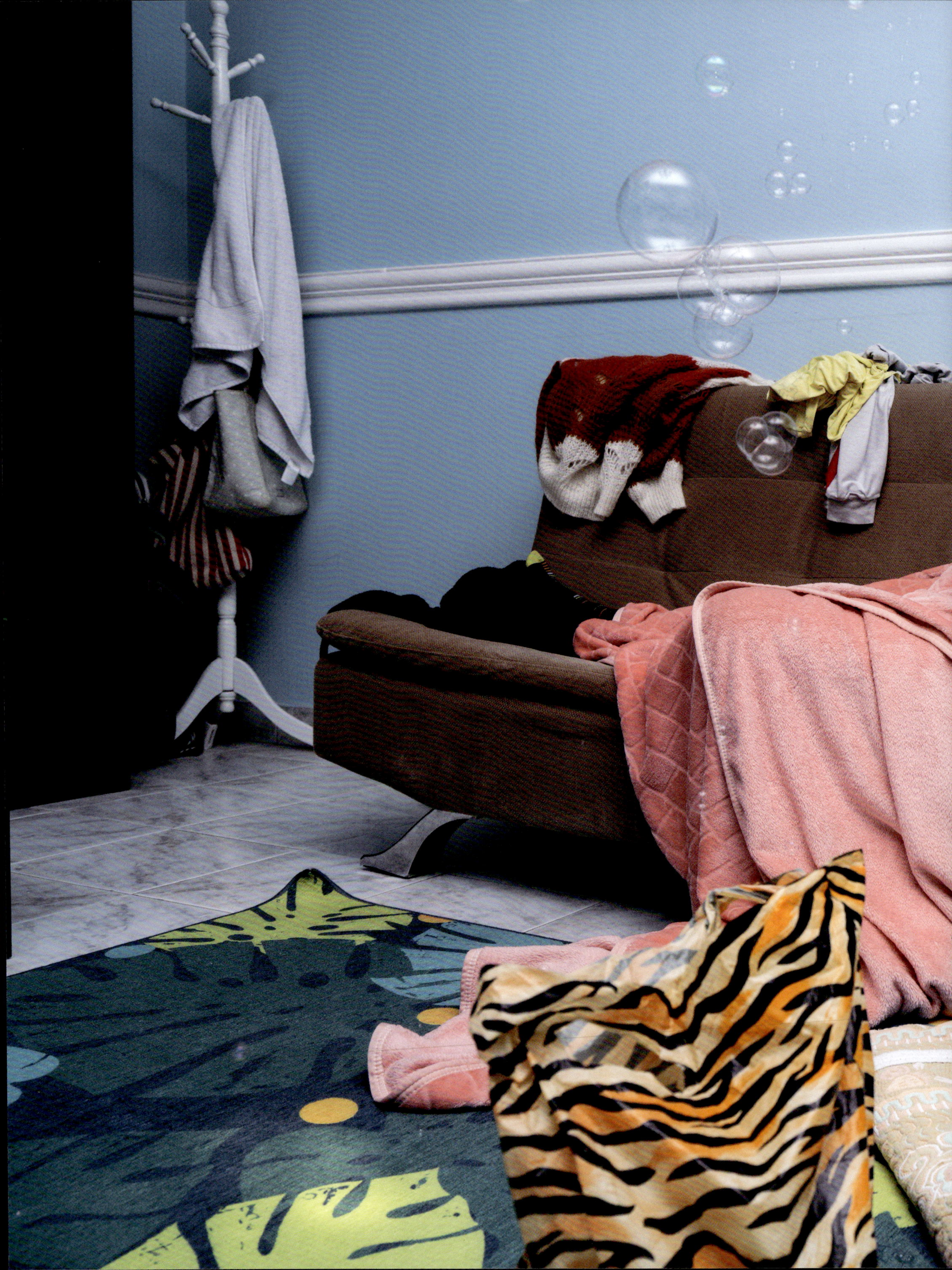

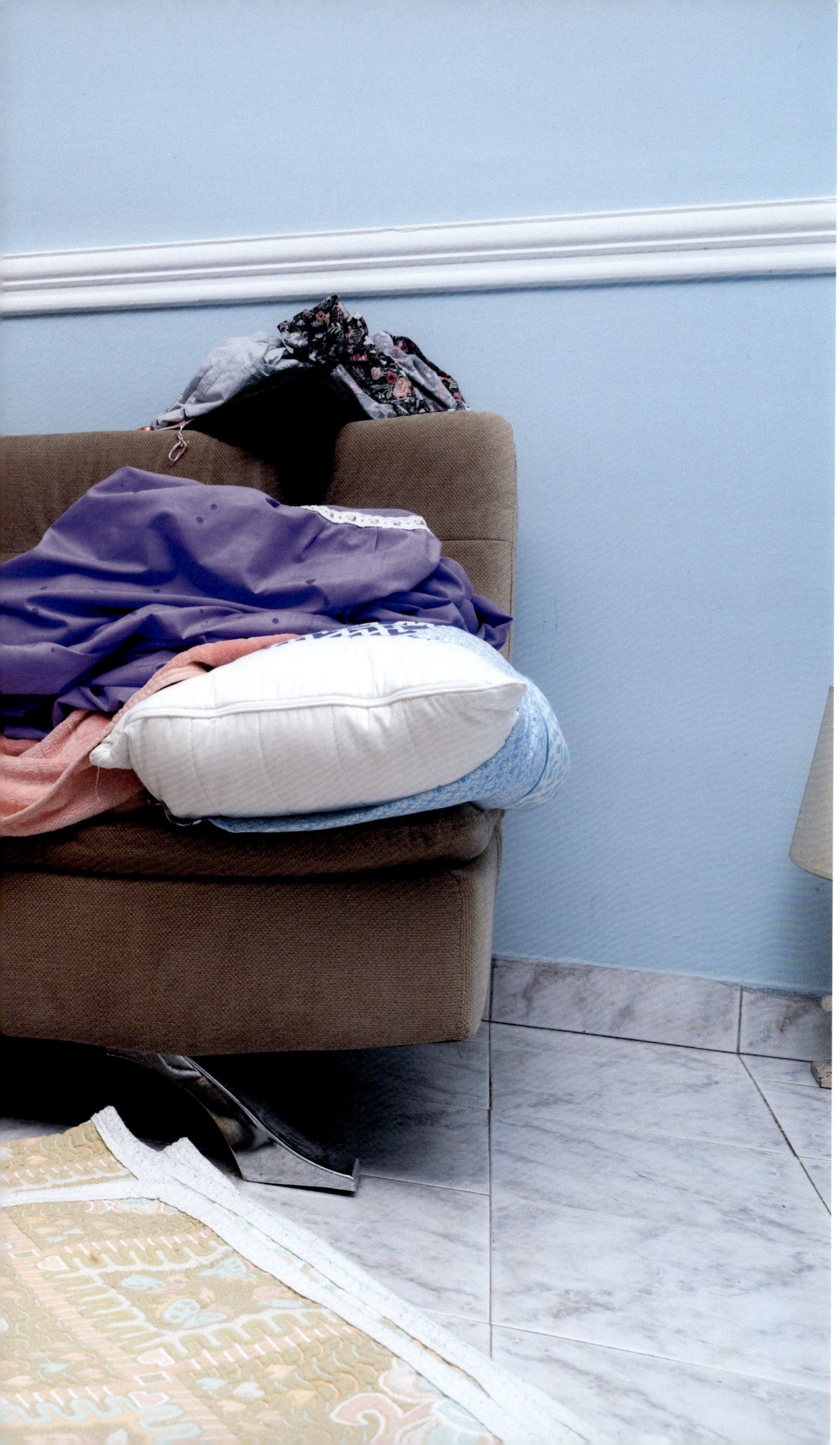

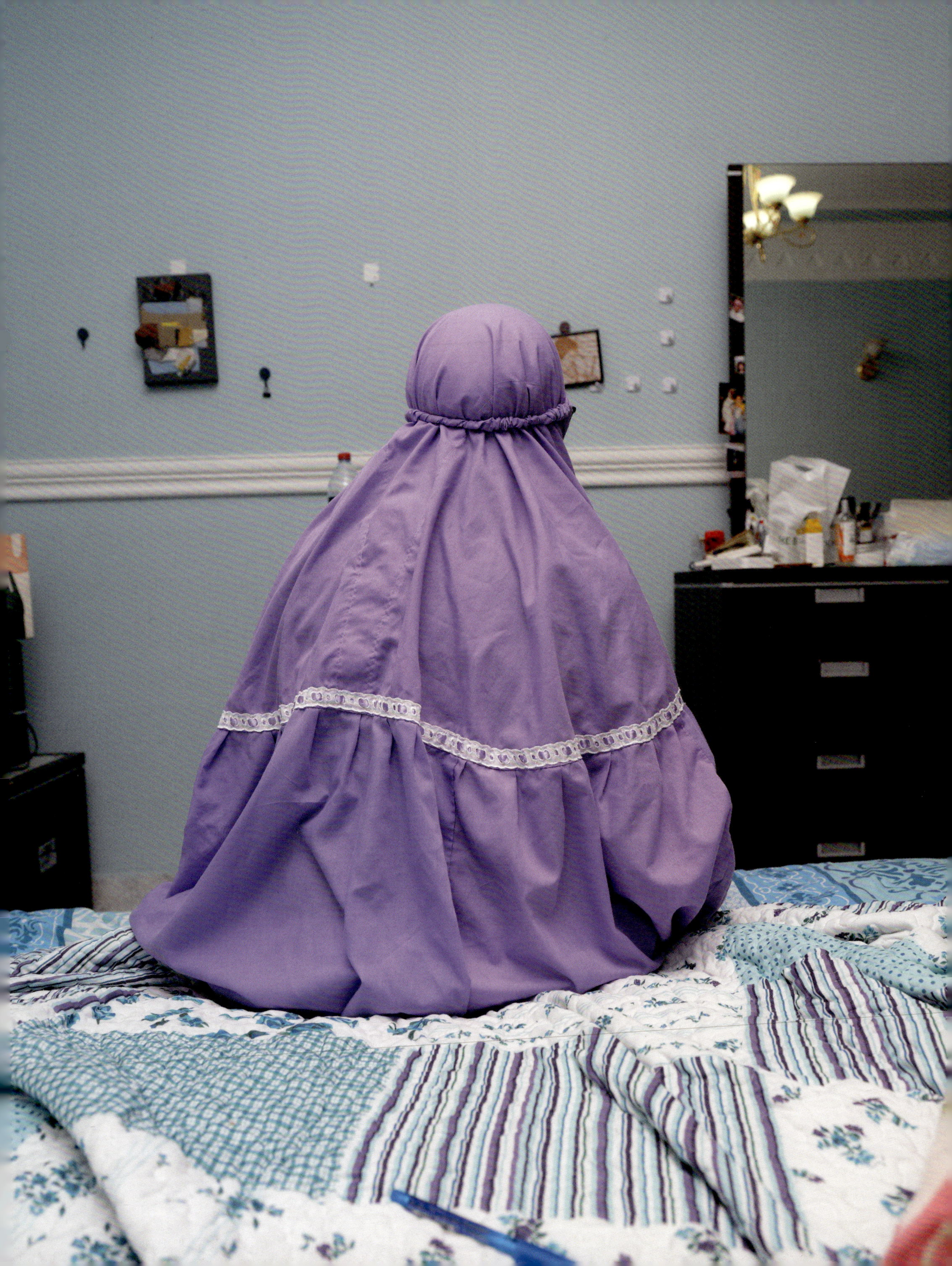

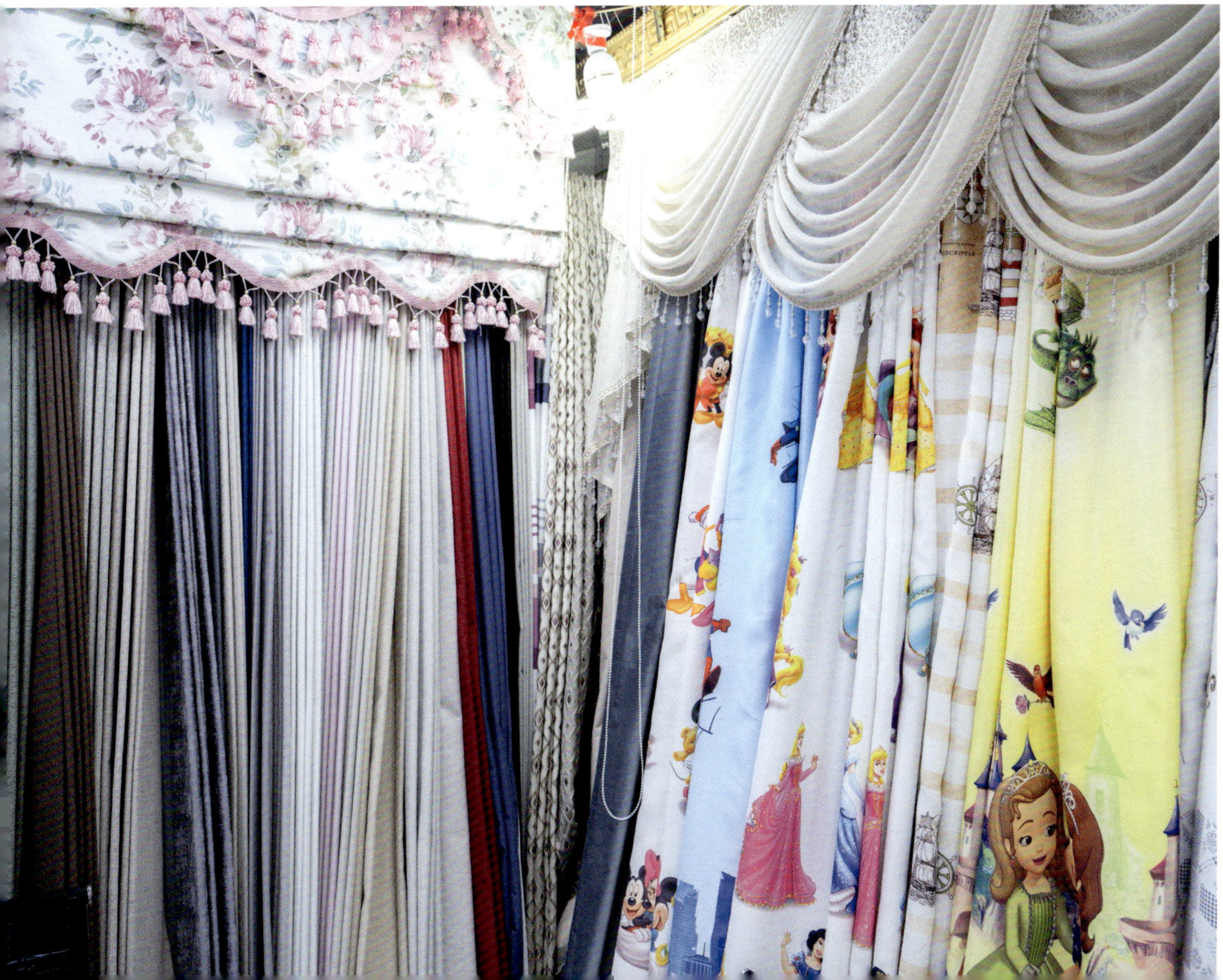

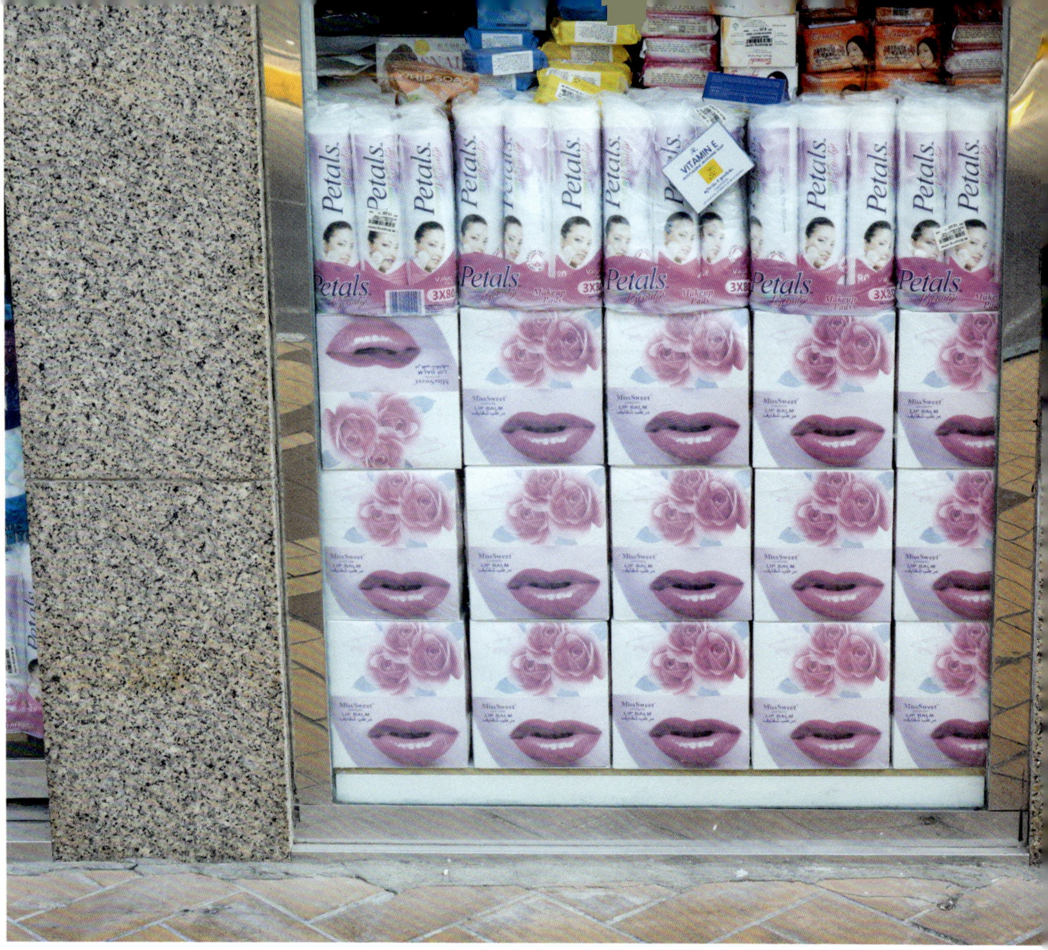
Petals
VITAMIN E
3X80

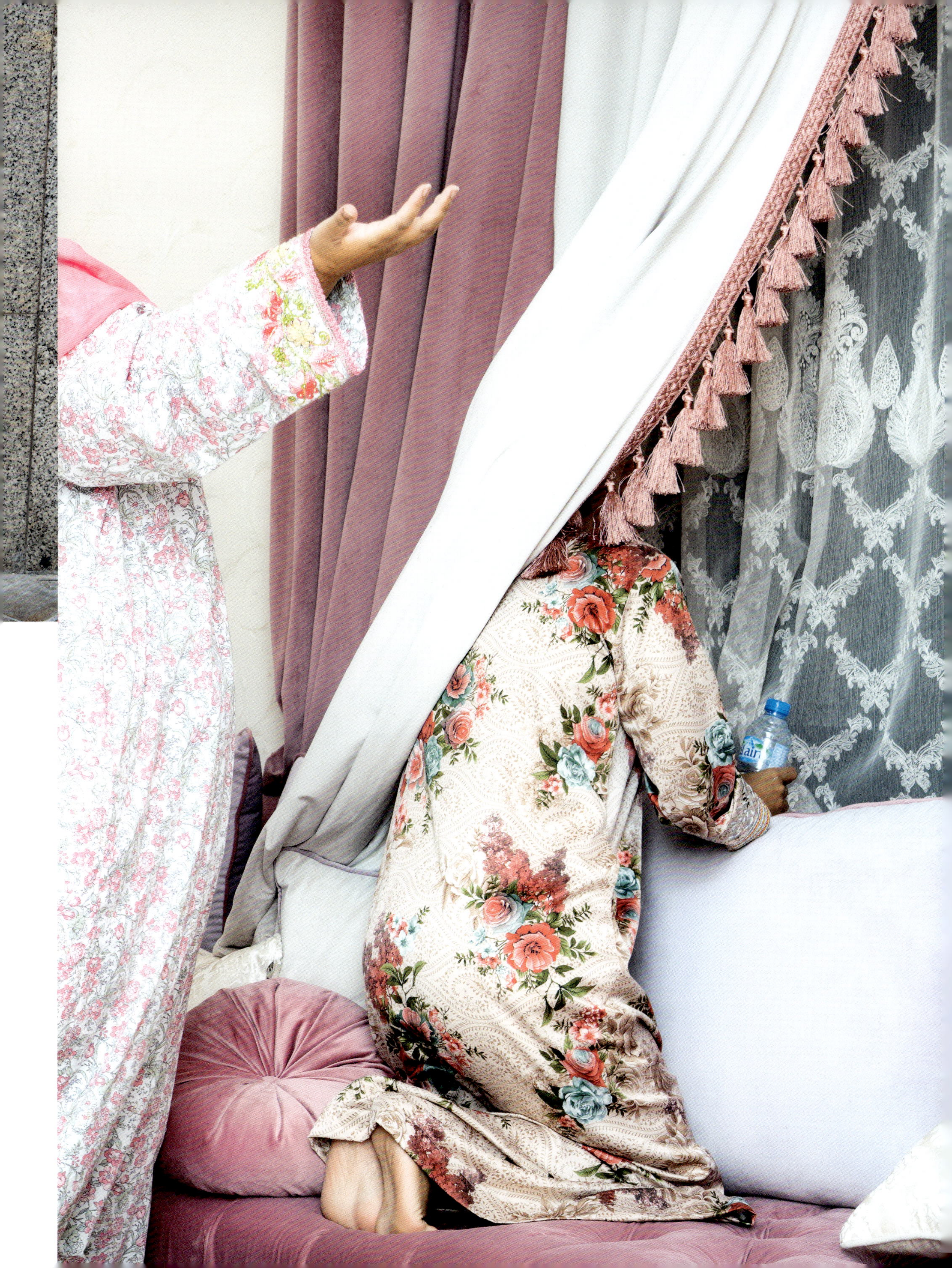

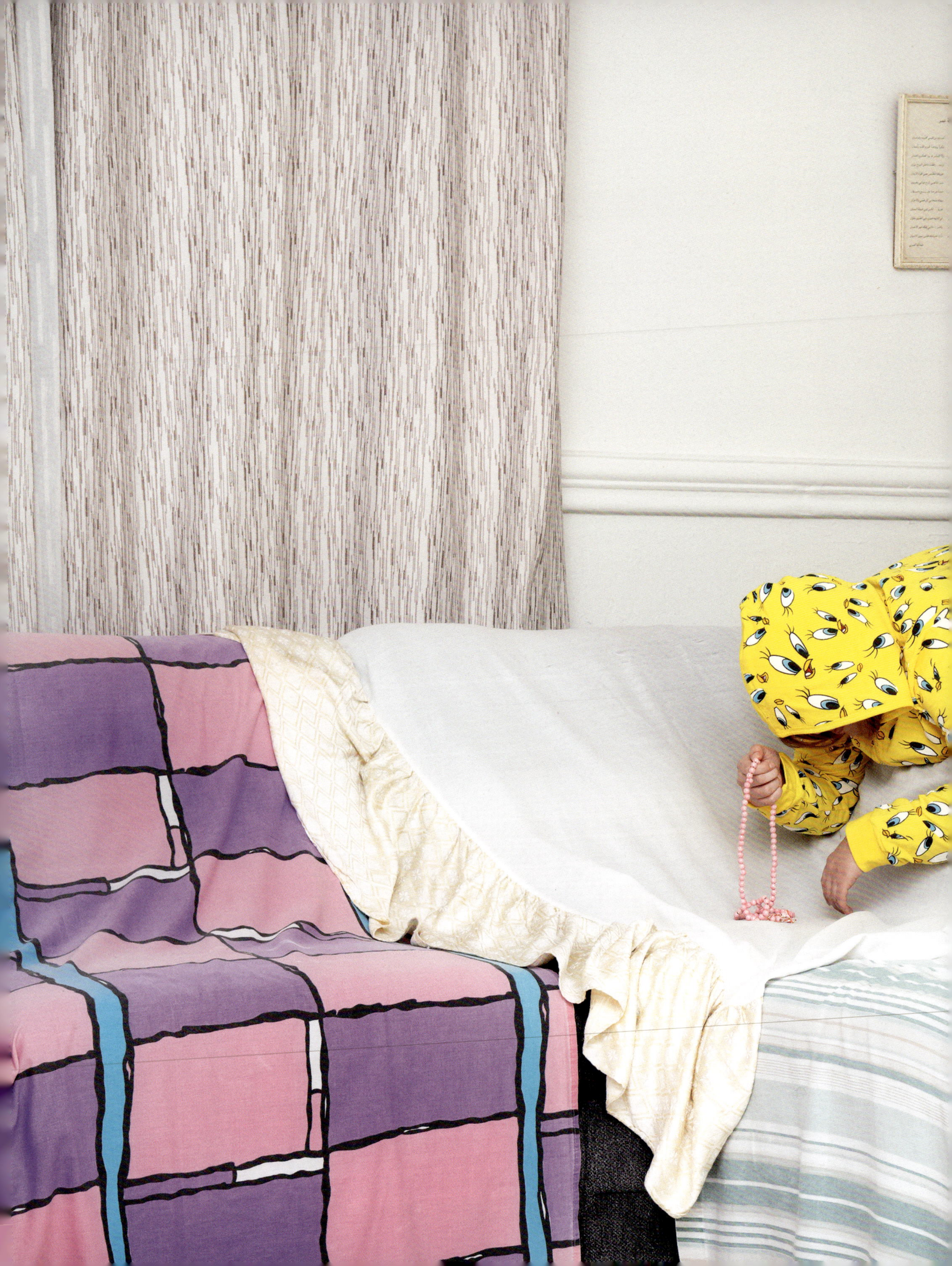

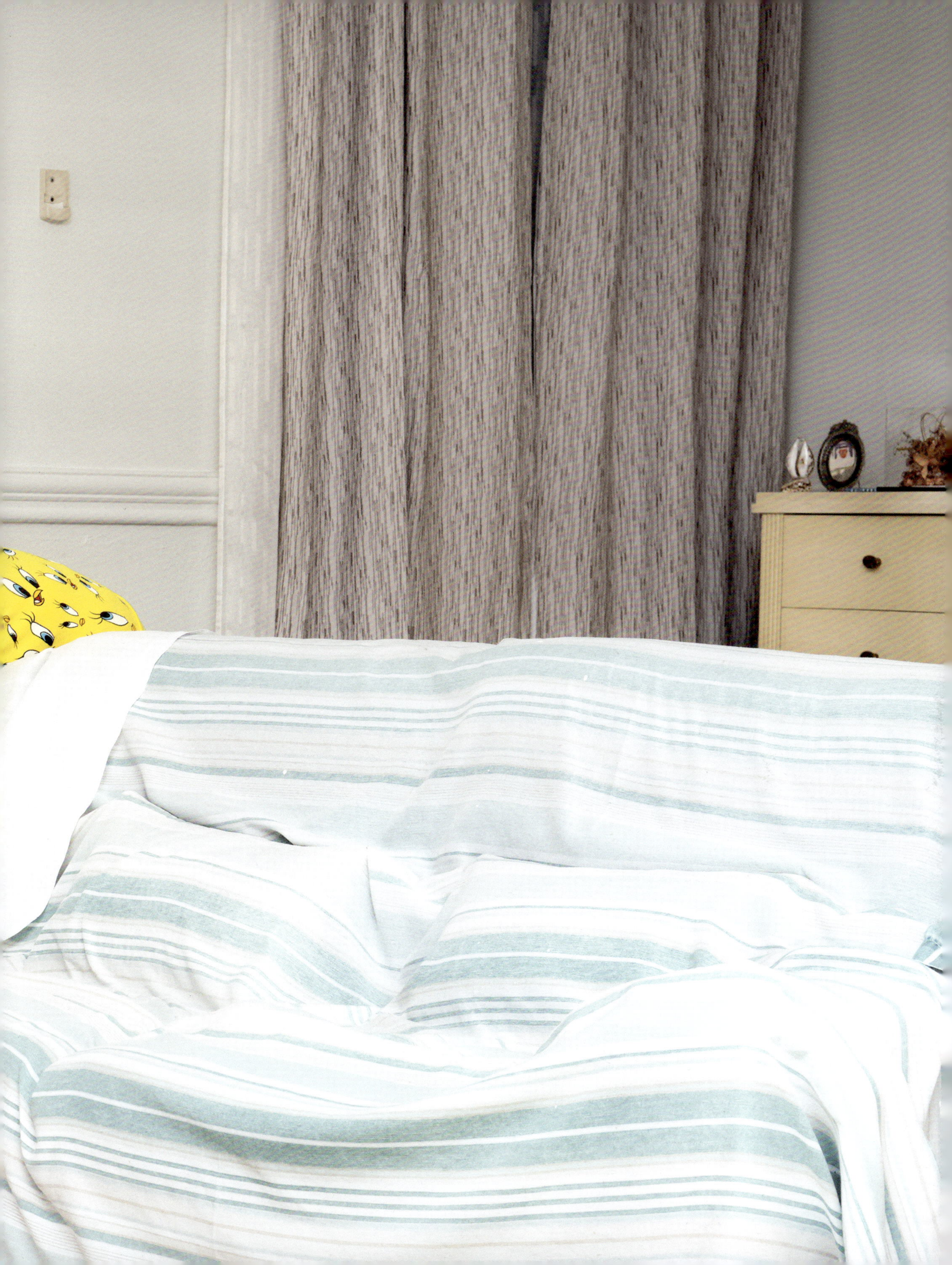

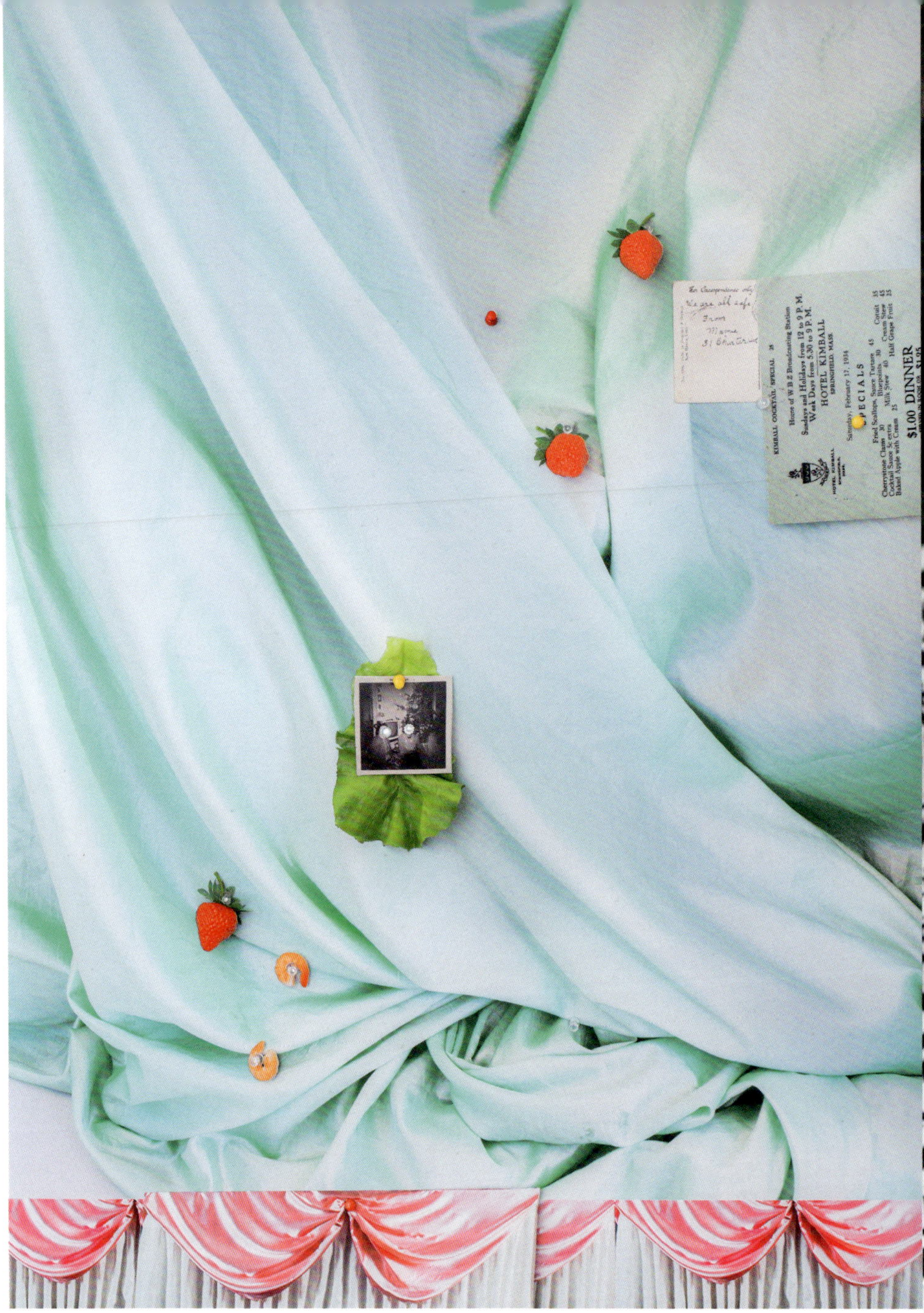
HOTEL KIMBALL
$1.00 DINNER
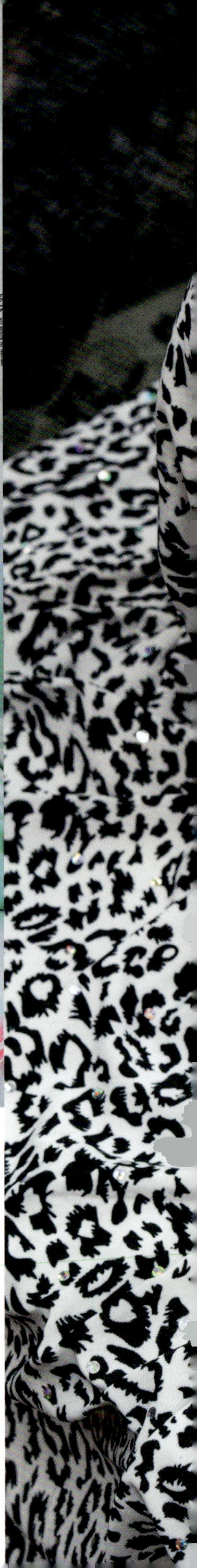

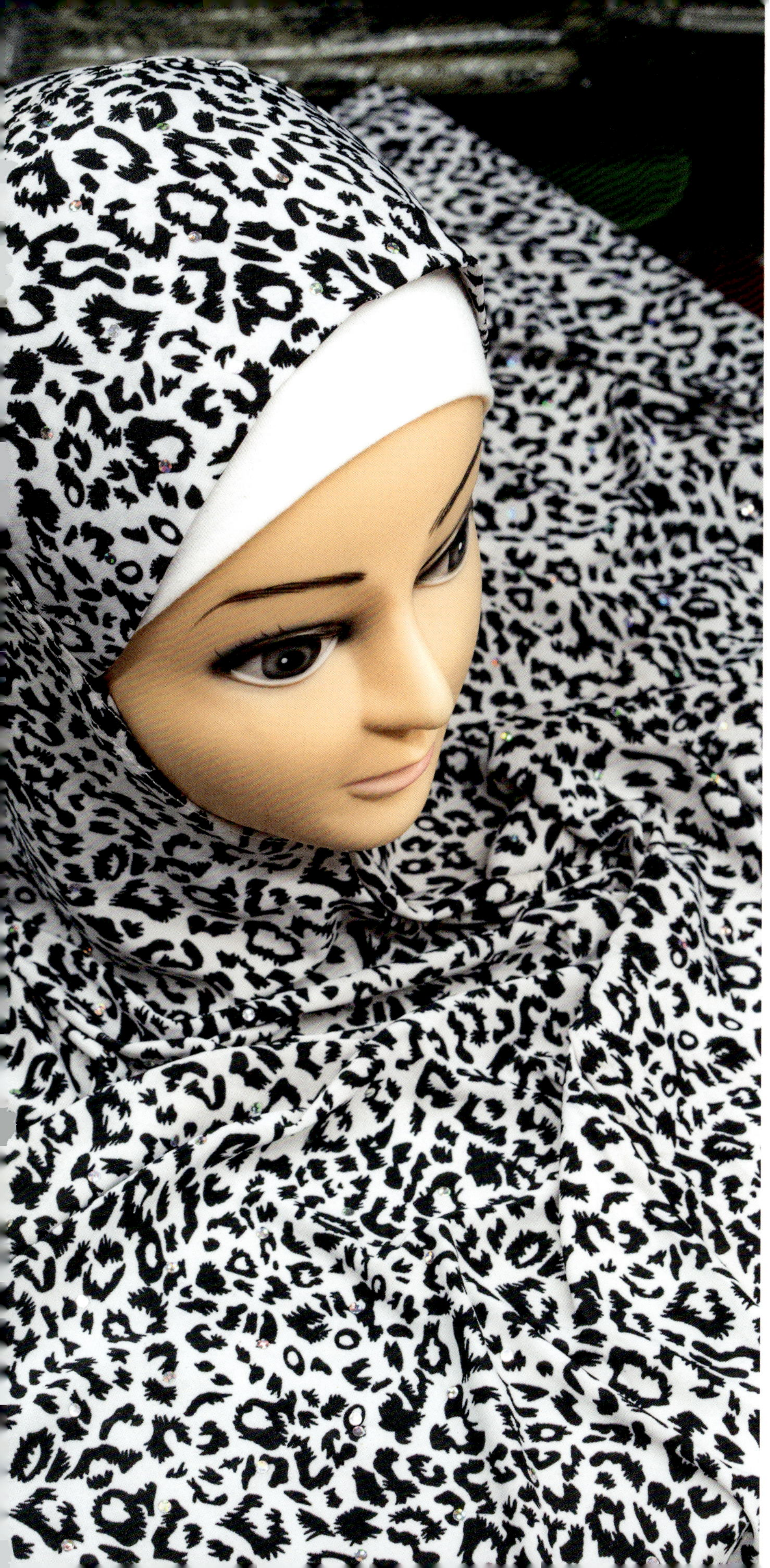

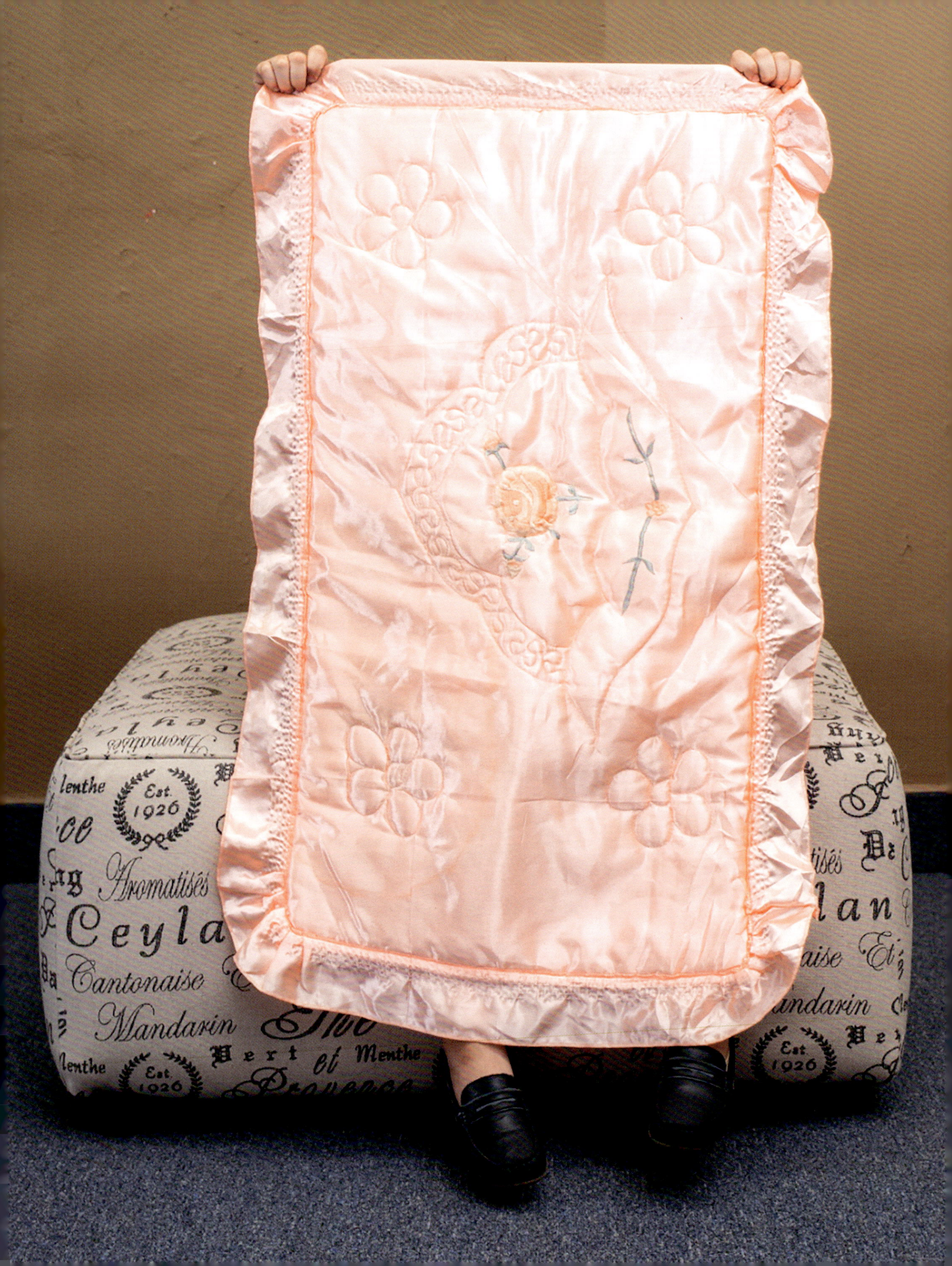

Est. 1926
Aromatisés
Ceyla
Cantonaise
Mandarin
Vert et Menthe
Est. 1926

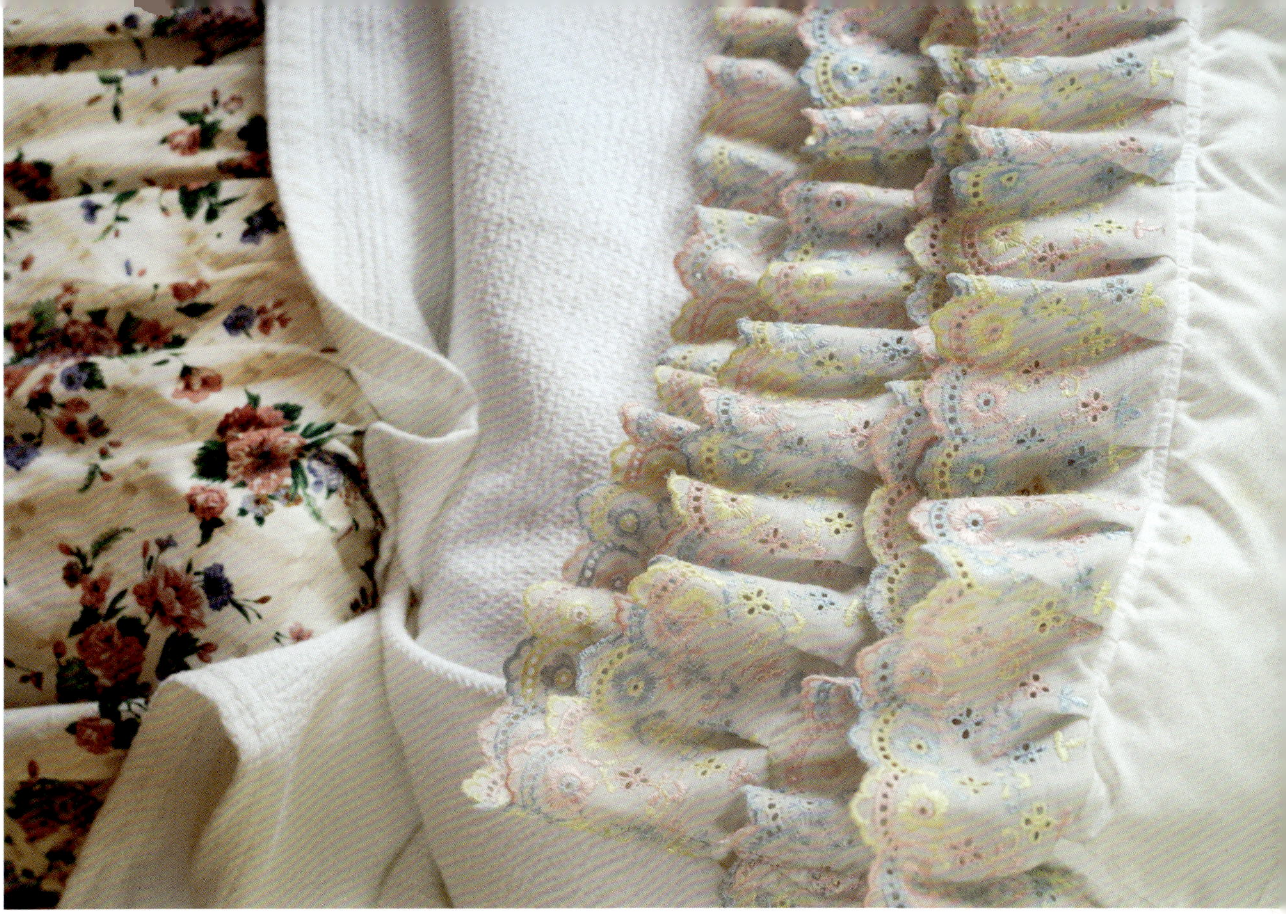

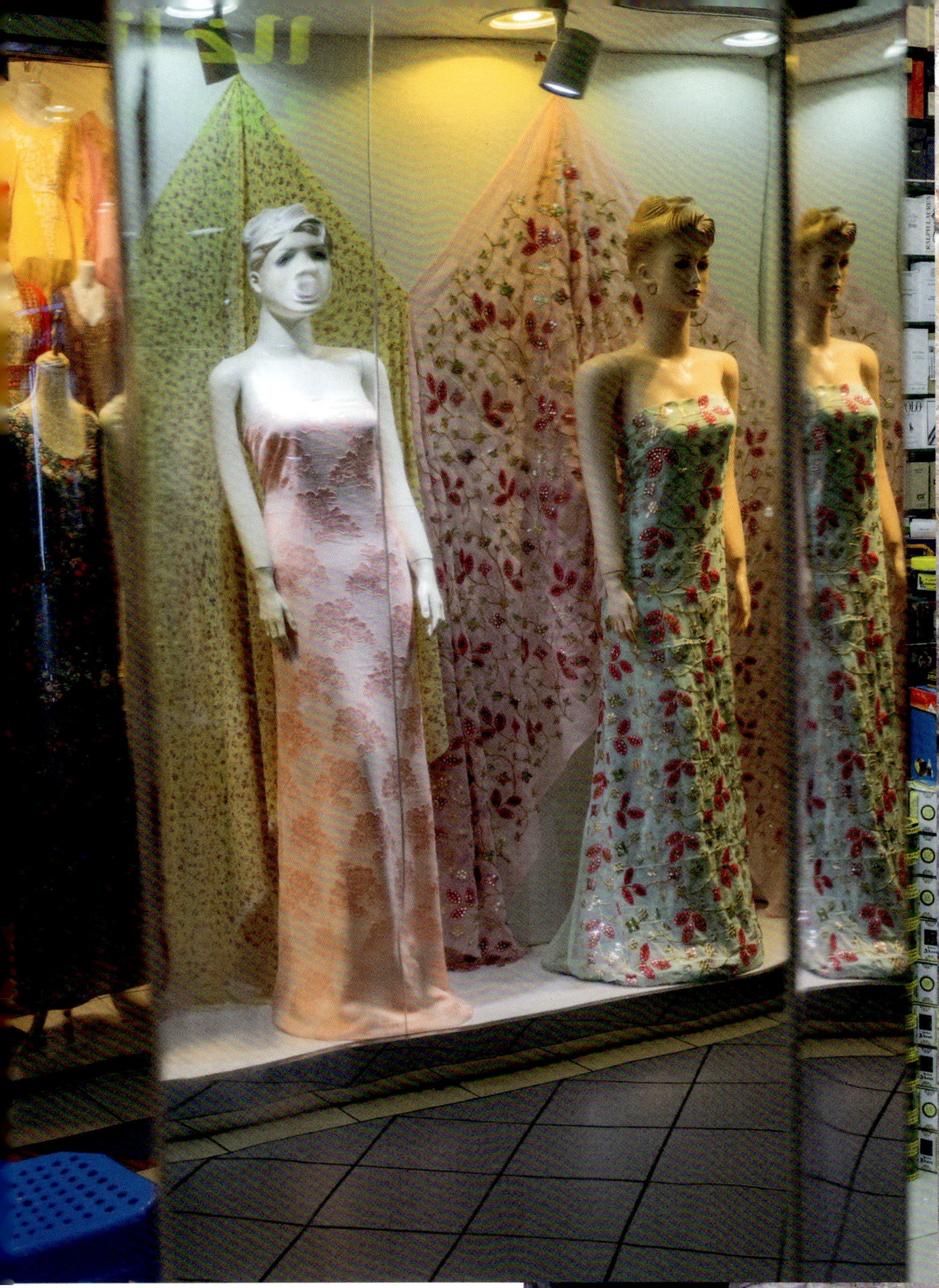

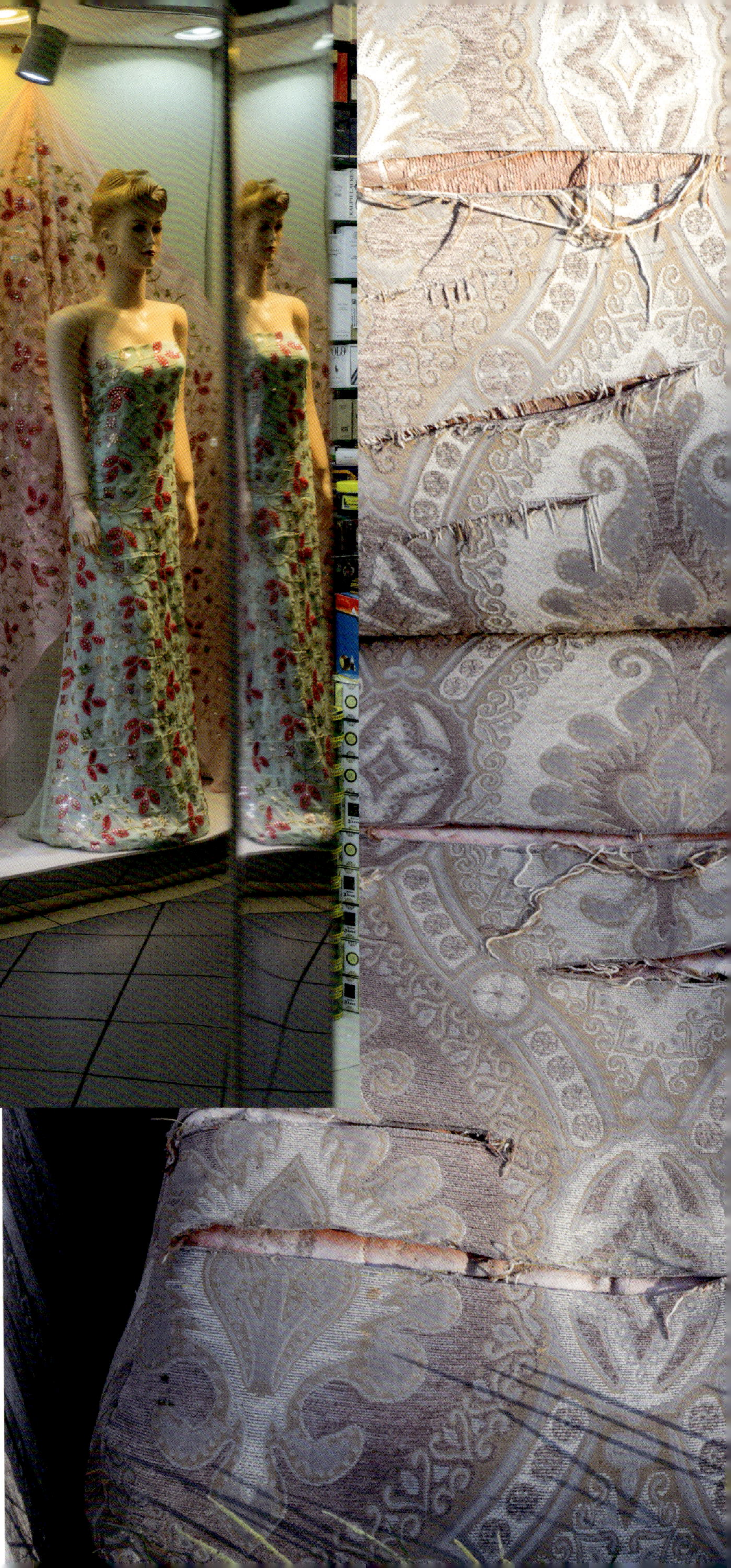

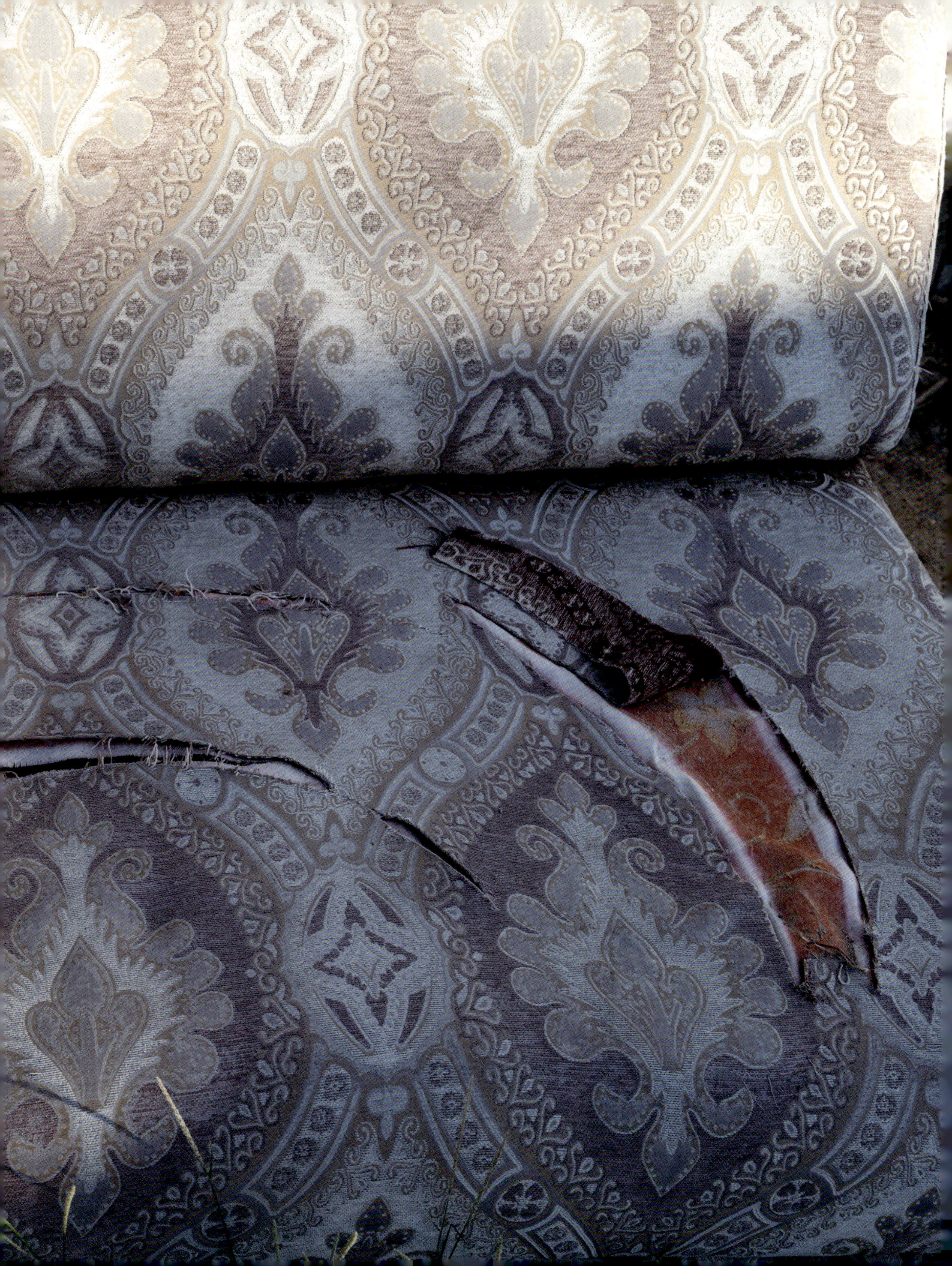

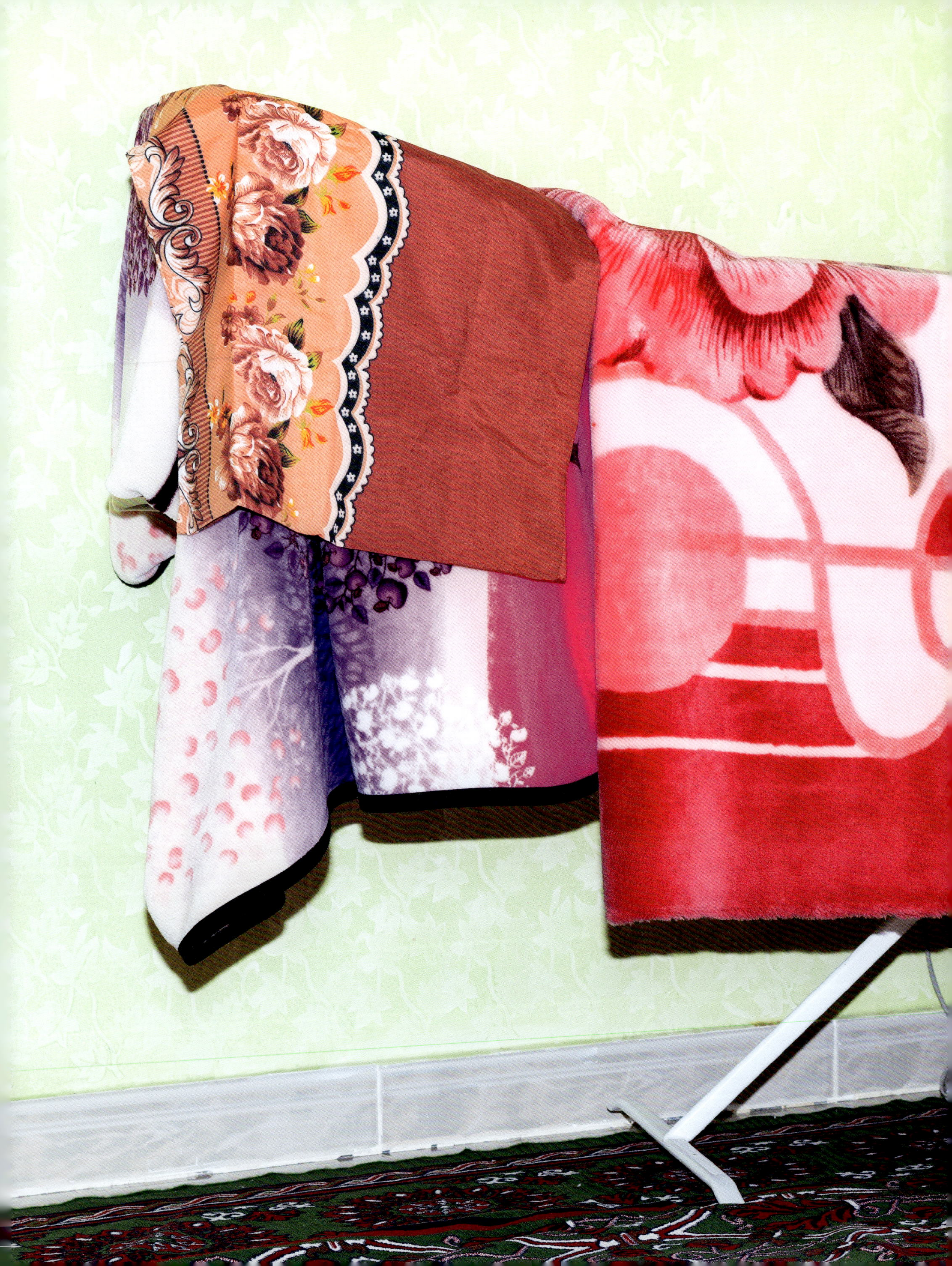

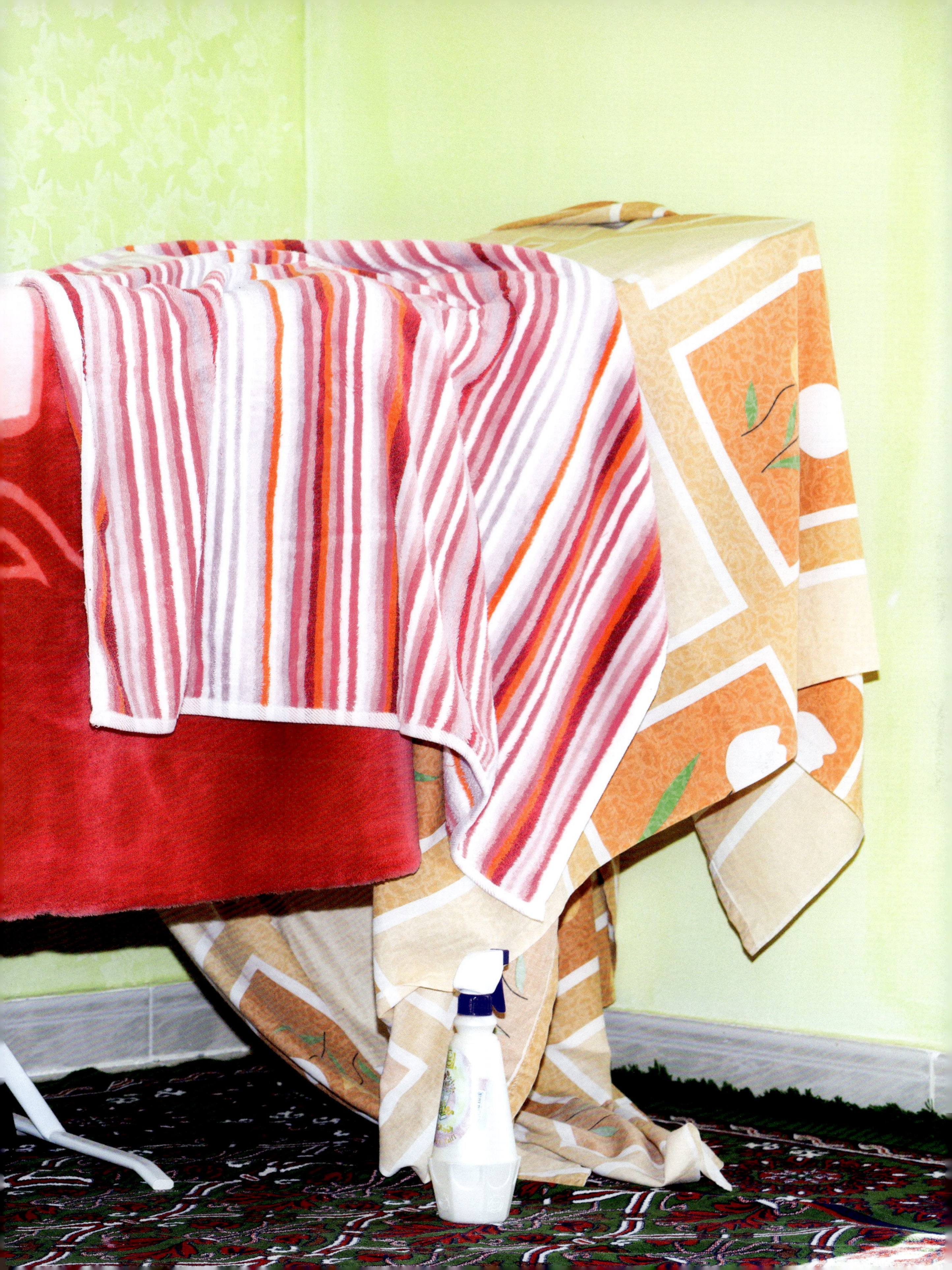

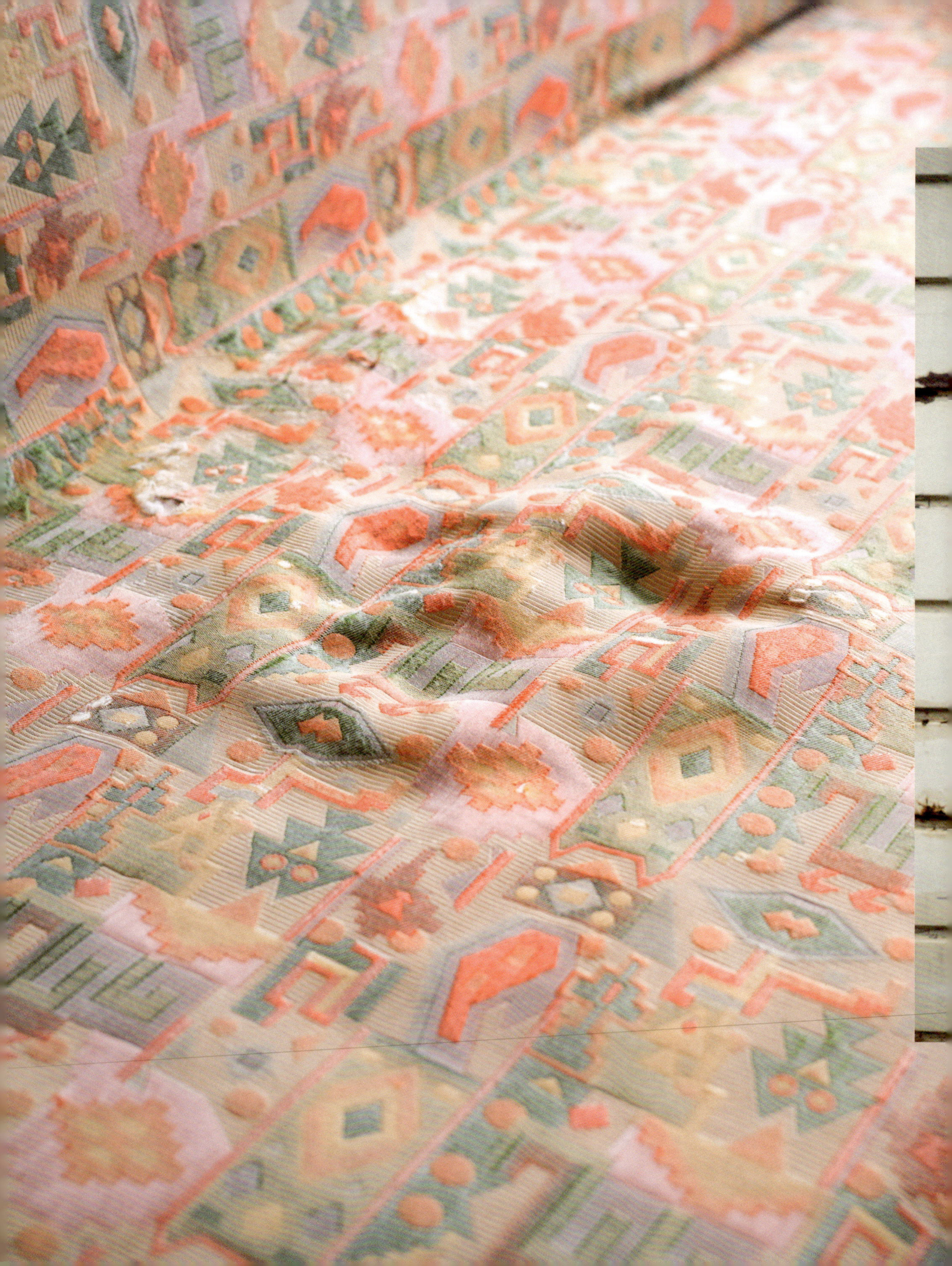

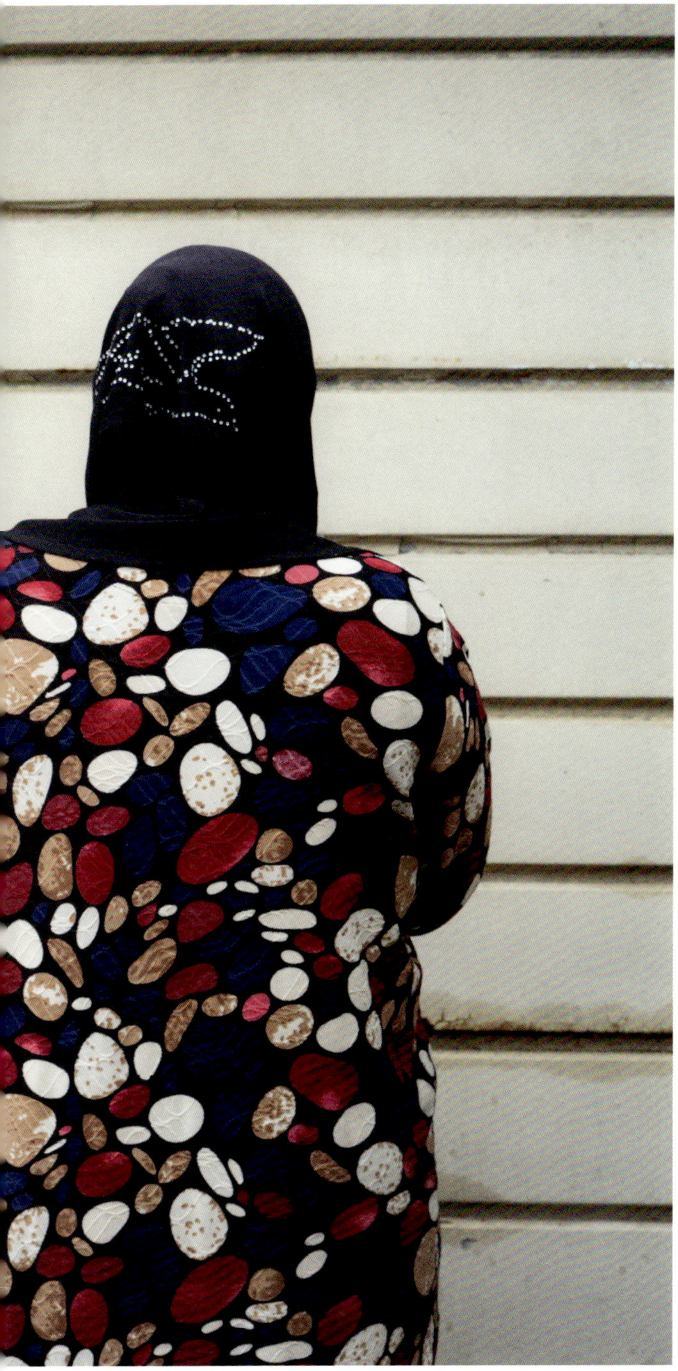

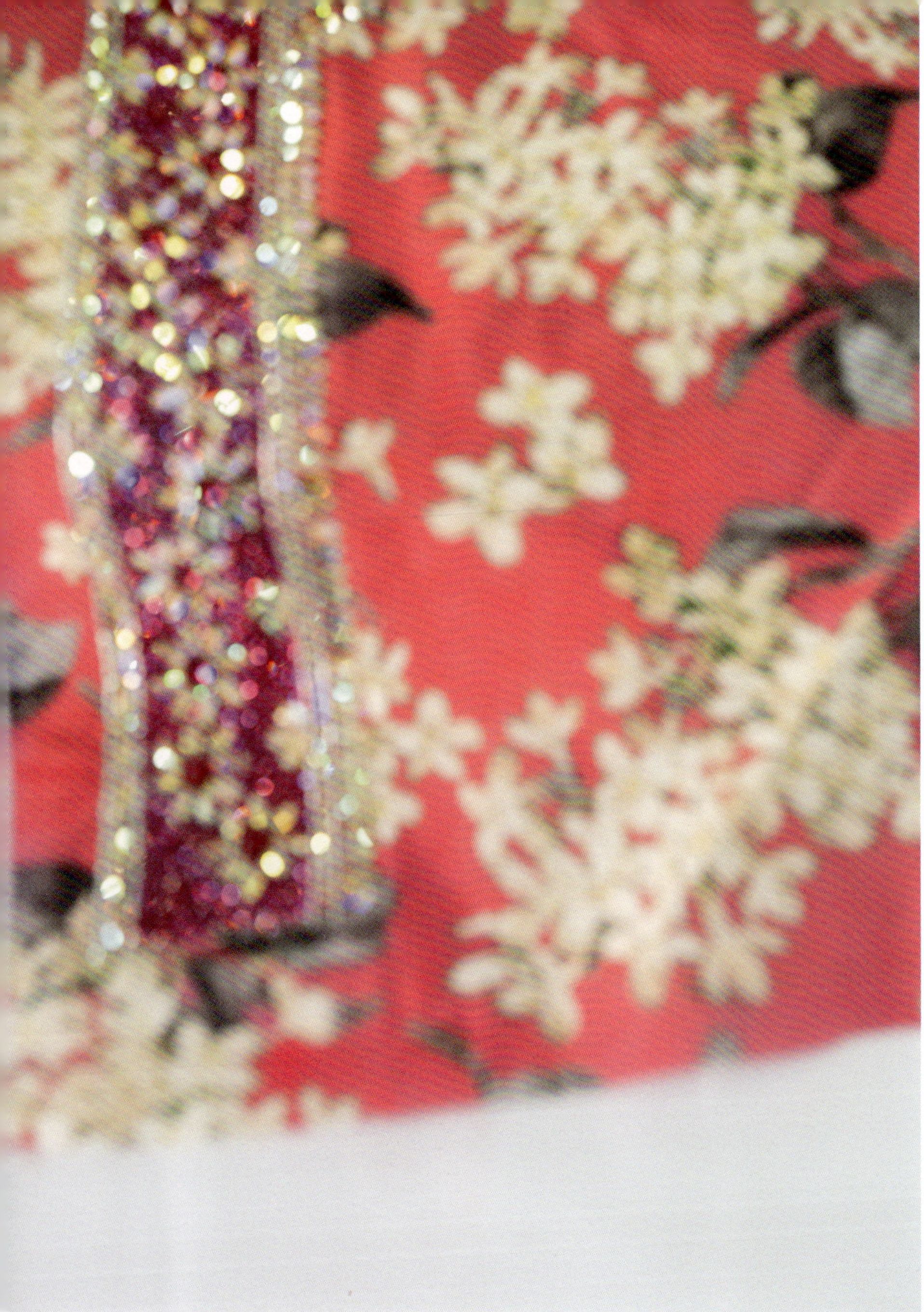

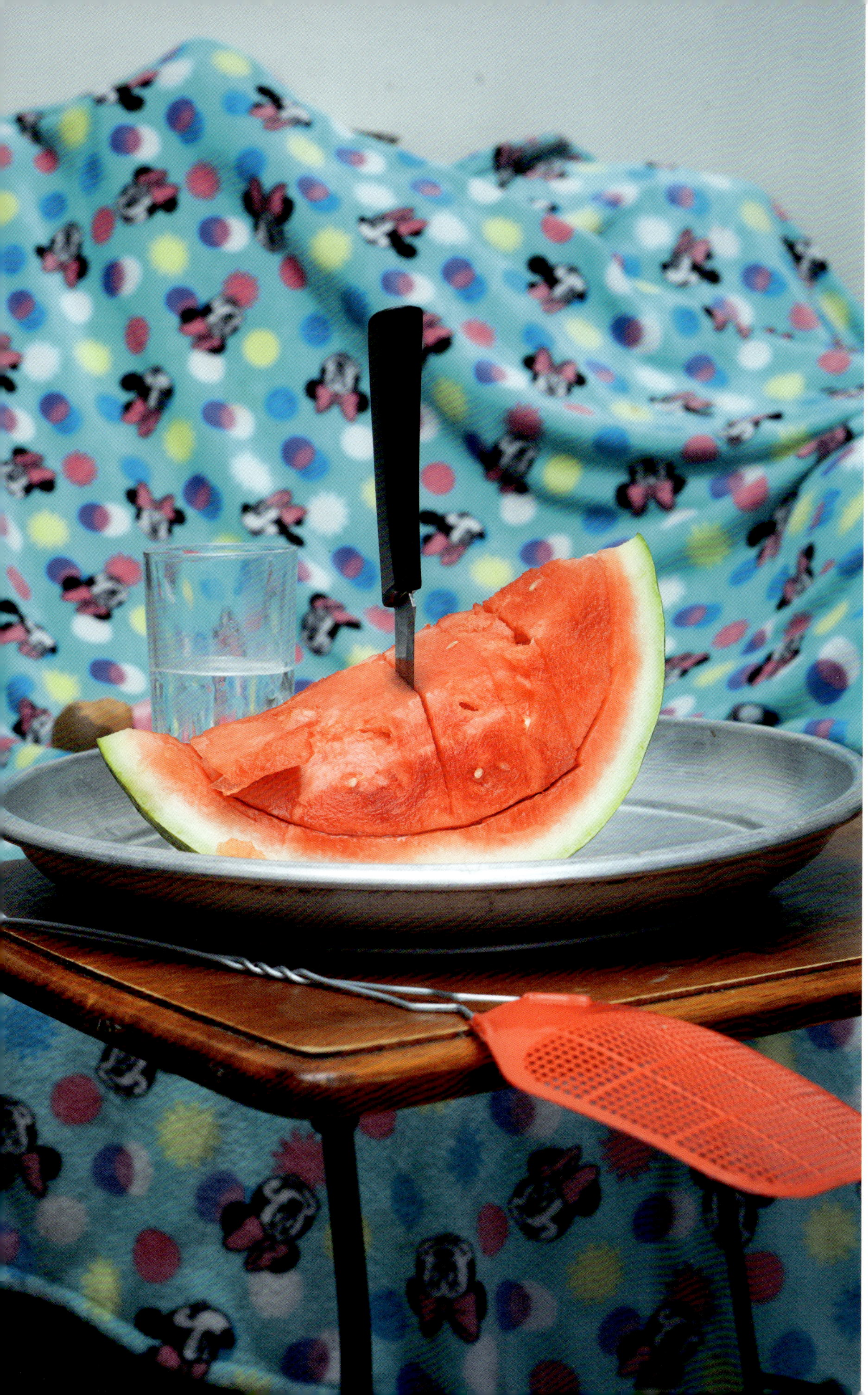

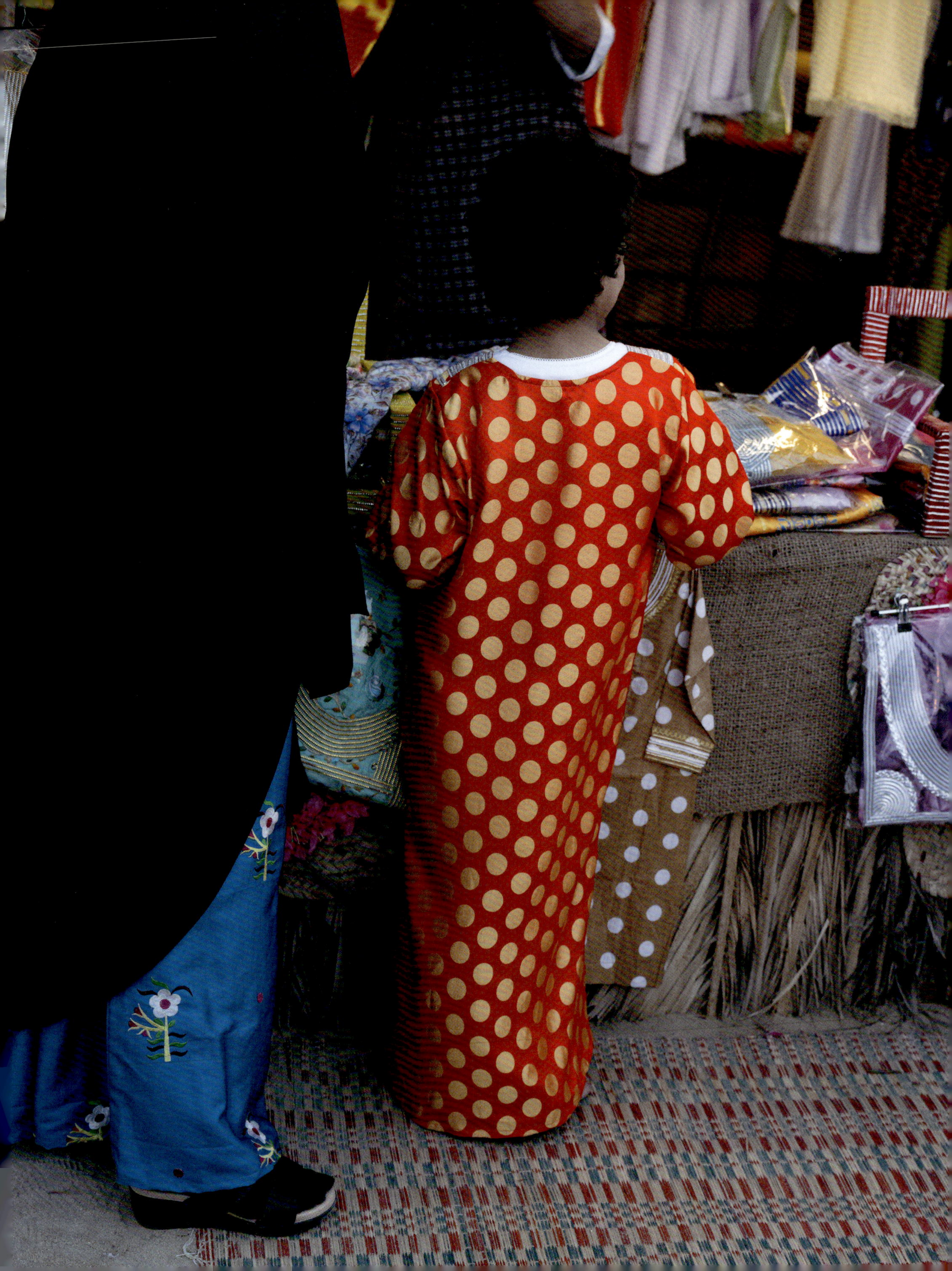

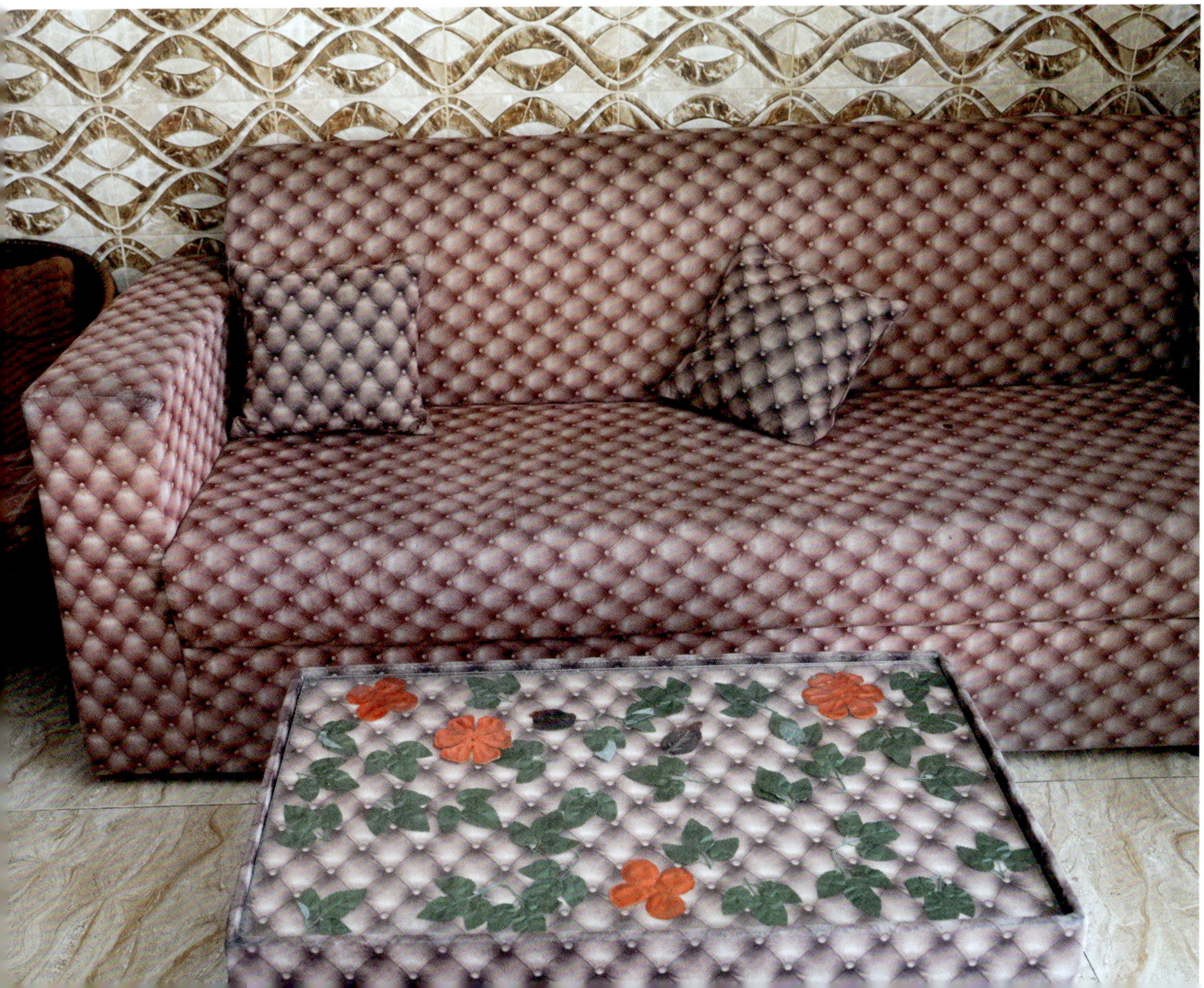

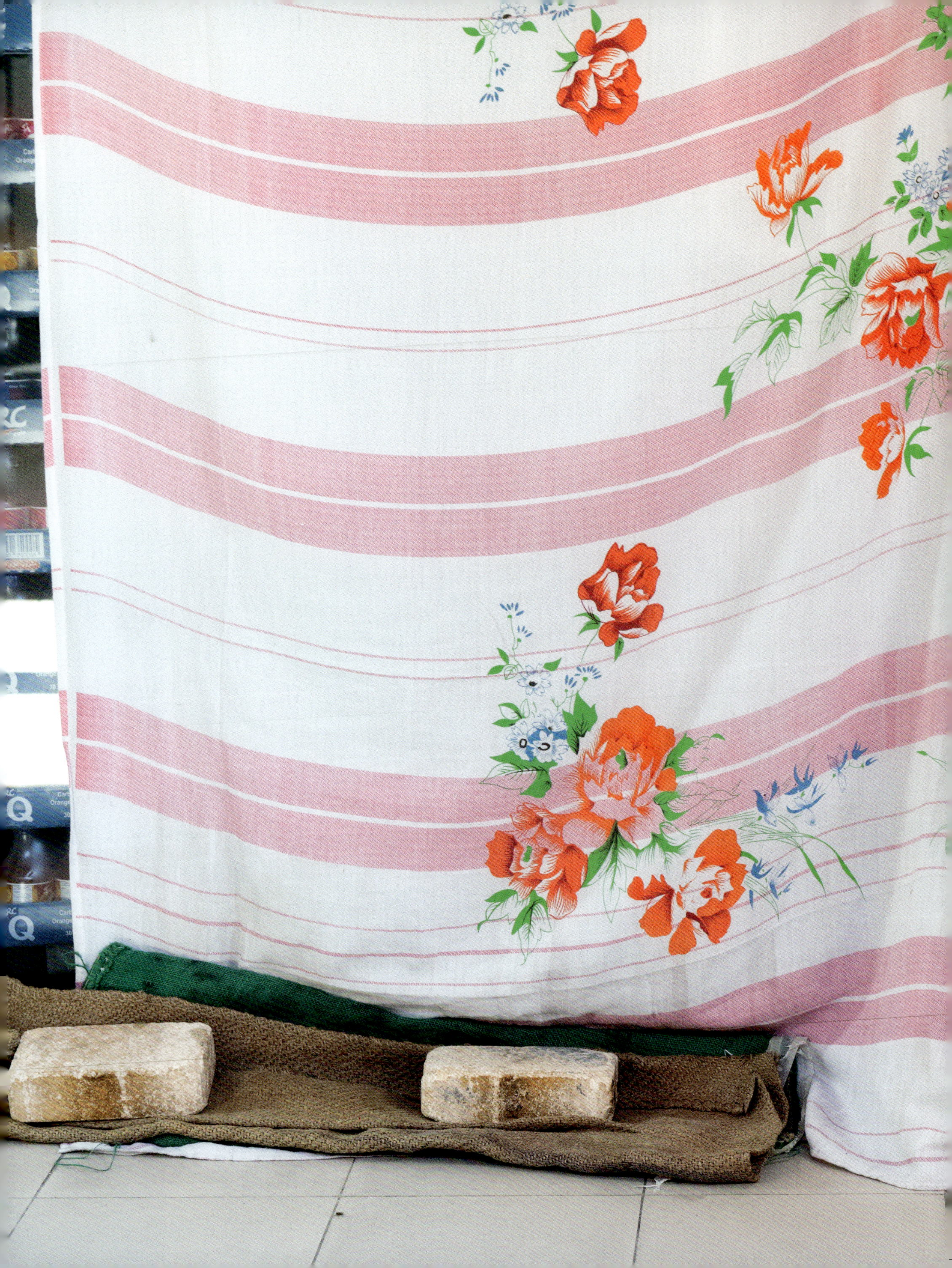

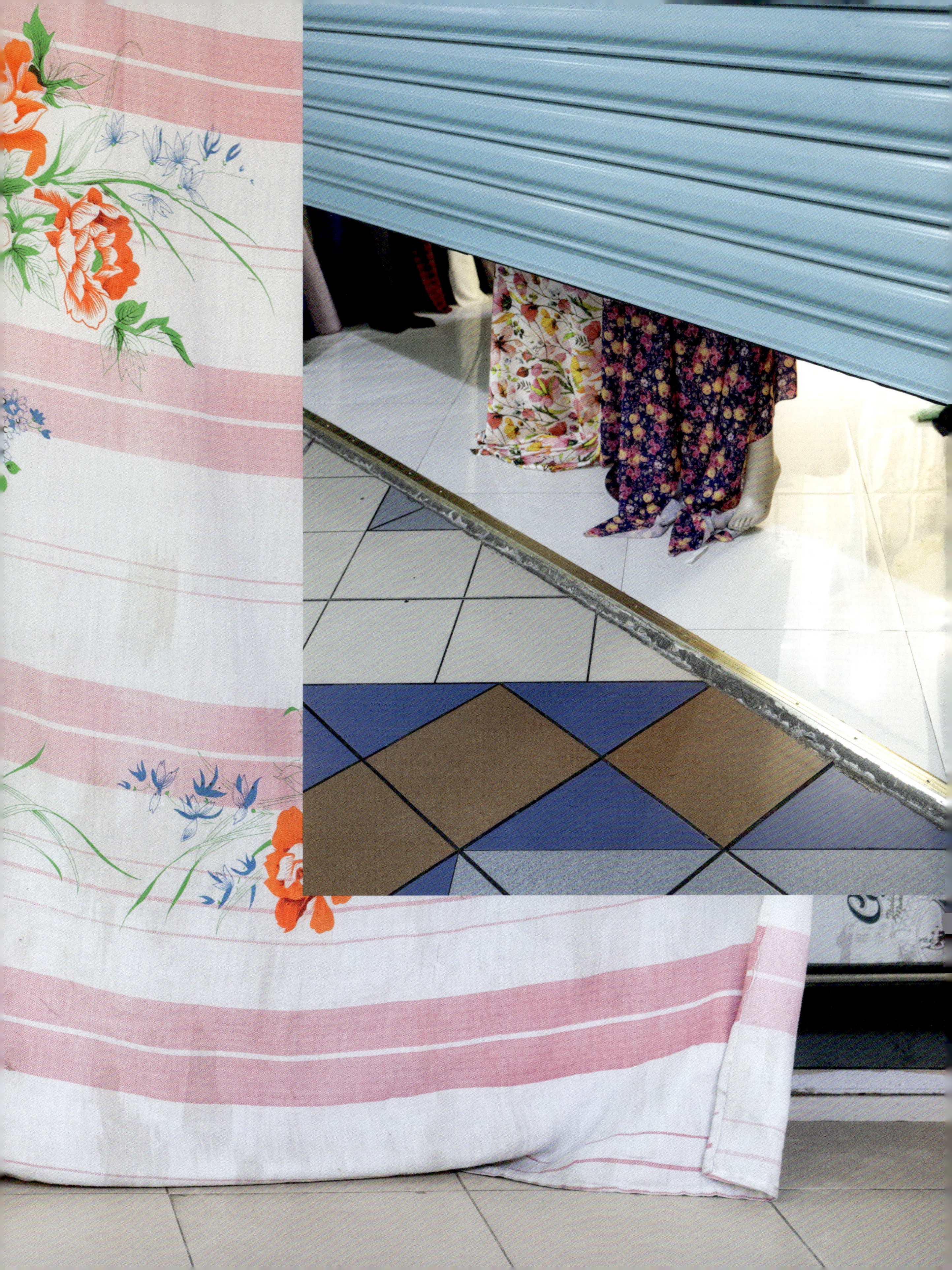

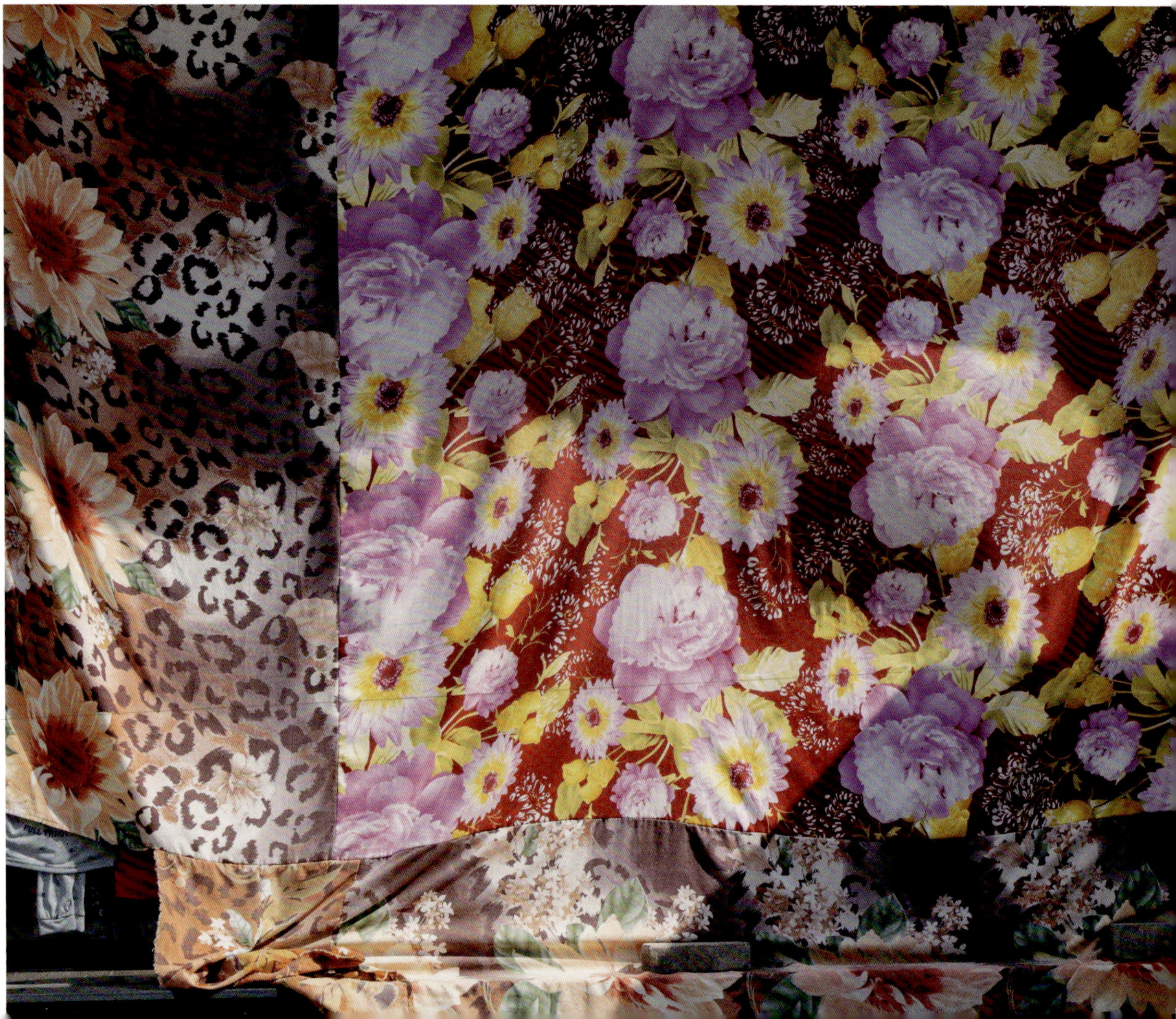

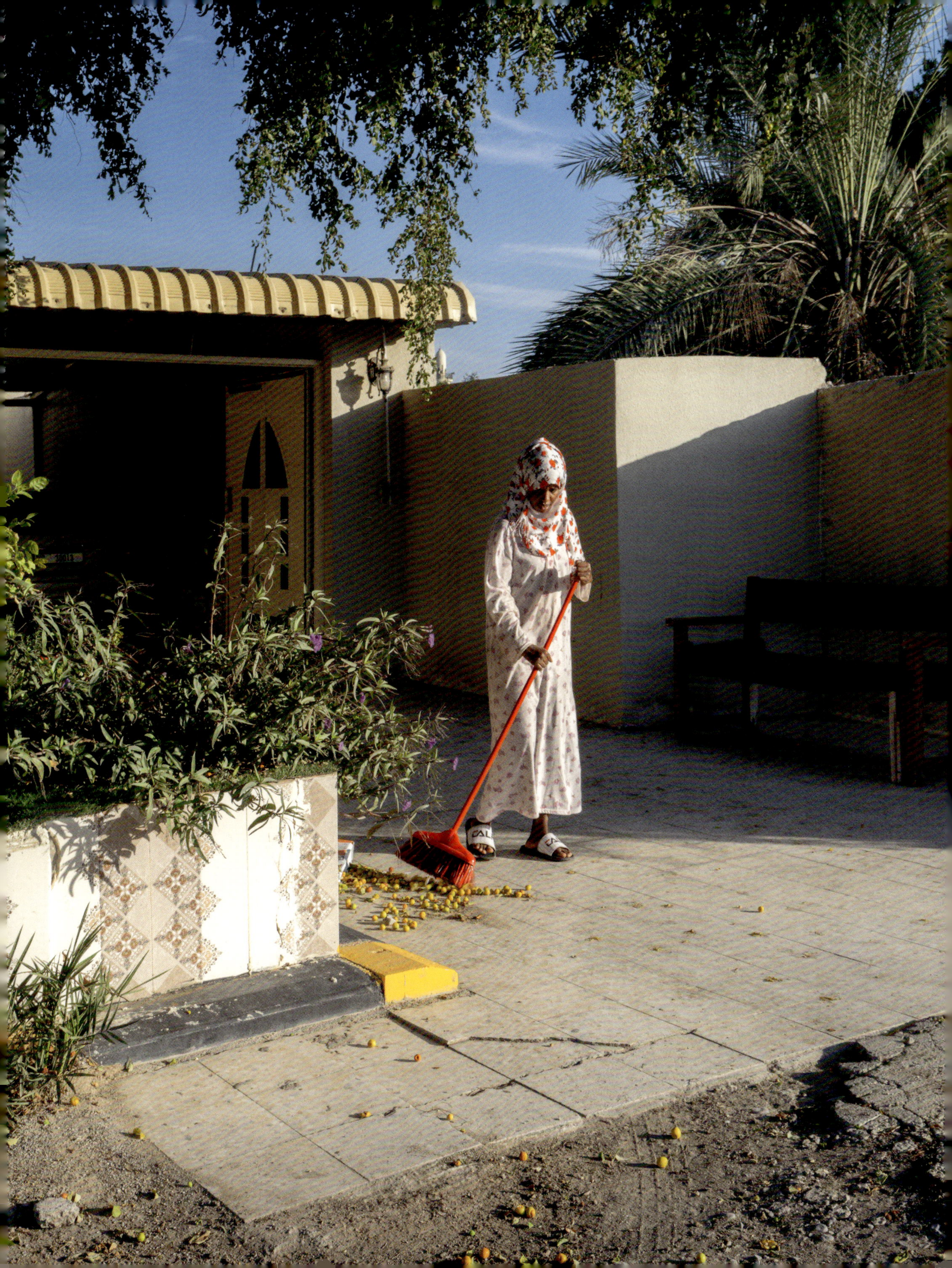

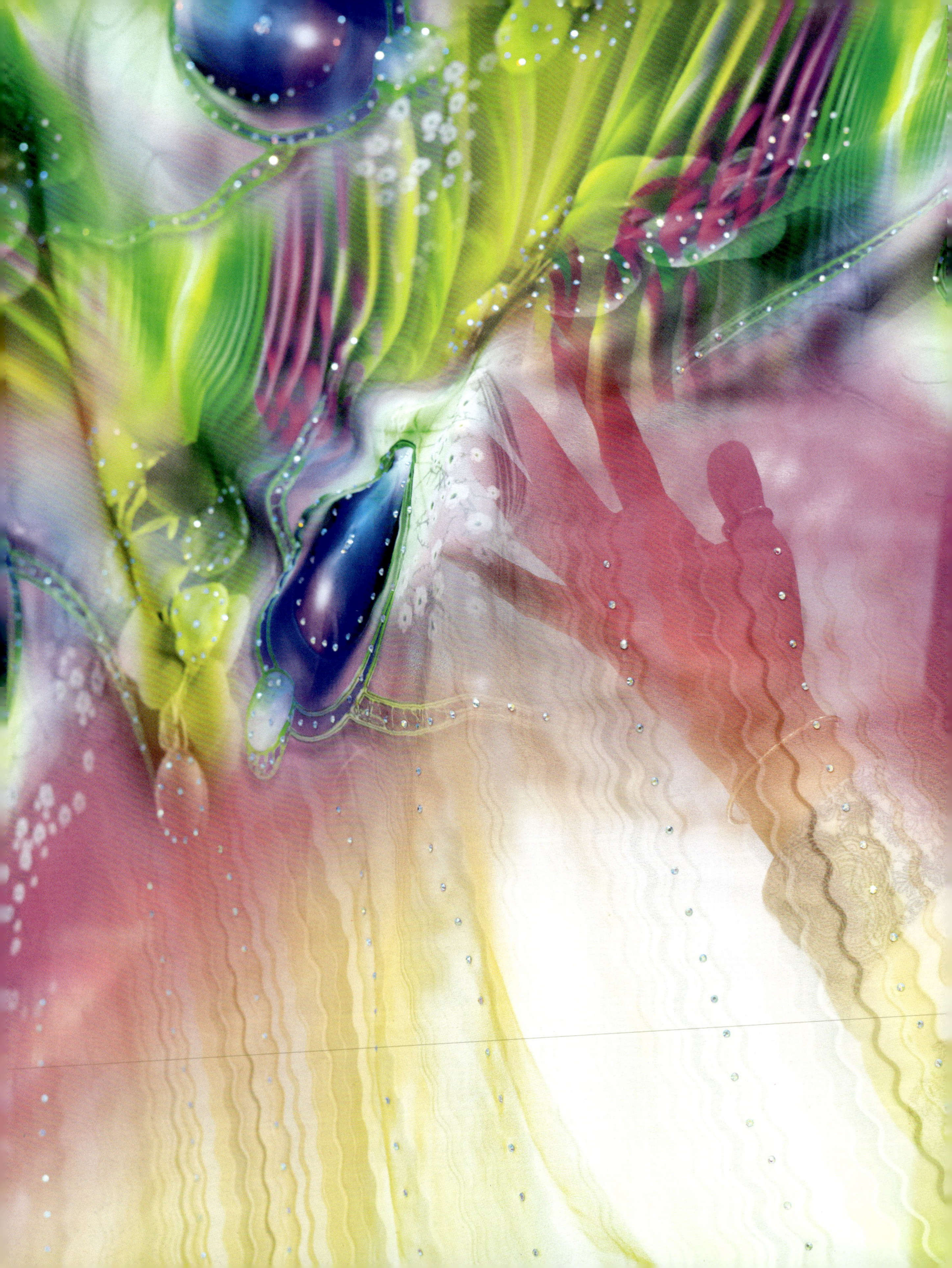